What Readers Are Saying
Grails 2: A Quick-Start G

This book is a delight: a warm, smart introduction to the Grails framework, illustrated by a friendly mentor over several iterations on a small project. It's pair-programming on the page. By the end of the ride, we've created an impressive app, and we're ready for deeper dives, with a wealth of resources provided. Fabulous!

➤ **Michael Easter**
   Software composer, codetojoy.blogspot.com

If you are looking for a book to take you from Java to productivity with Grails as quickly as possible, this is your book. Dave has produced a fantastic and pragmatic iterative guide to building a full Grails application, including advice for development and production. This book is the quickest way to accelerate your learning of Grails.

➤ **Ken Sipe**
   CTO, Code Mentor, Inc.

Dave and Ben have done it again. *Grails 2: A Quick Start Guide* is the best book you could hand to a new Grails developer. It's a great mix of instruction and practice and just what you need to get started, or get better, with Grails.

➤ **Jared Richardson**
   Agile coach, Agile Artisans

Grails 2: A Quick-Start Guide

Dave Klein
Ben Klein

The Pragmatic Bookshelf

Dallas, Texas • Raleigh, North Carolina

Many of the designations used by manufacturers and sellers to distinguish their products are claimed as trademarks. Where those designations appear in this book, and The Pragmatic Programmers, LLC was aware of a trademark claim, the designations have been printed in initial capital letters or in all capitals. The Pragmatic Starter Kit, The Pragmatic Programmer, Pragmatic Programming, Pragmatic Bookshelf, PragProg and the linking *g* device are trademarks of The Pragmatic Programmers, LLC.

Every precaution was taken in the preparation of this book. However, the publisher assumes no responsibility for errors or omissions, or for damages that may result from the use of information (including program listings) contained herein.

Our Pragmatic courses, workshops, and other products can help you and your team create better software and have more fun. For more information, as well as the latest Pragmatic titles, please visit us at *http://pragprog.com*.

The team that produced this book includes:

Susannah Davidson Pfalzer (project manager)
Potomac Indexing, LLC (indexer)
David J Kelly (typesetter)
Janet Furlow (producer)
Juliet Benda (rights)
Ellie Callahan (support)

Printed in the United States of America.
ISBN-13: 978-1-937785-77-2
Printed on acid-free paper.
Book version: P1.0—December 2013

Contents

Greetings and Salutations! ix

1. **Enough Groovy to Be Dangerous** 1
   Groovy Syntax Compared to Java   1
   Groovy Strings   3
   Groovy Closures   4
   Groovy Collections   5
   Metaprogramming   9
   Where to from Here?   10

2. **Our Project** 11
   Introducing TekDays.com   11
   Meet Our Customer   12
   Iteration Zero   14
   Summary   20

3. **Laying the Foundation** 21
   Creating a Domain Class   21
   More About Domain Classes   23
   Testing Our Domain Class   24
   Taking Control of Our Domain   27
   Modifying Code That Doesn't Exist   28
   Bootstrapping Some Test Data   32
   Summary   35

4. **Building Relationships** 37
   The TekUser Domain Class   37
   One-to-One Relationships   40
   One-to-Many Relationships   44
   Collections of Simple Data Types   46
   Adding a Sponsor Class   48
   Many-to-Many Relationships   49

Finishing Up the Domain Model 54
Summary 57

5. **Beyond Scaffolding** **59**
Generating Scaffolding Code 59
Anatomy of a Grails Controller 60
Grails Views with Groovy Server Pages 66
Configuring a Database 79
Summary 83

6. **Getting Things Done** **85**
Changing All Our Views at Once 85
Modifying the Scaffolded Views 86
Event Task List 94
Grails Service Classes 94
Integration Testing 98
Modifying the Task Class 100
Summary 101

7. **Forum Messages and UI Tricks** **103**
Restricting Messages to an Event 103
Of Templates and Ajax 108
Display Message Threads with a Custom Tag 116
Summary 120

8. **Knock, Knock: Who's There? Grails Security** **121**
Grails Security Options 121
Logging In 121
Filters 125
Logging Out 128
Summary 130

9. **Big-Picture Views** **131**
Home Page Makeover 131
Creating a New Controller 135
Designing the Dashboard View 135
Adding the Dashboard Action 142
Adding a Menu 143
Linking to the Dashboard 145
Summary 146

10. **Seek, and You Shall Find** **147**
    Search Using Dynamic Finders   147
    Hibernate Criteria Builder   151
    The Big Guns: The Searchable Plugin   153
    Summary   159

11. **Icing on the Cake** **161**
    The jQuery UI Plugin   161
    The Twitter4J Plugin   166
    User-Friendly URLs   169
    Summary   172

12. **Deployment and Beyond** **173**
    Using a JNDI Data Source   173
    Creating and Deploying a WAR   176
    Next Steps   176
    Parting Thoughts   177

A1. **Additional CSS Rules** **179**

A2. **Resources** **181**
    Online Resources   181
    Meet the GR8 Community   182
    Other Resources   186
    IDE Support   187

    Bibliography **189**

    Index **191**

Greetings and Salutations!

Let Me Tell You About Grails...

Web development is a rewarding experience. Building an application that can run from anywhere in the world is pretty awesome. Even in a corporate environment, you can deliver new features to your users, no matter where they are located, without ever touching their computer. It's a beautiful thing. Consider also what you can build: the potential for creativity on the Web is unlimited.

The Java platform brings even more power to the party. The Java Servlet API and the plethora of libraries and frameworks in the Java ecosystem make it possible to include almost any feature you could want in a web application. It is an exciting time to be a web developer. However, it's not all sweetness and light.

With all this power comes a level of complexity that can be daunting. With most Java-based web frameworks, there are multiple XML configuration files to deal with, along with classes to extend and interfaces to implement. As a project grows, this complexity seems to increase exponentially.

Many web application frameworks have been created to address this problem. So many Java web frameworks have been developed that you might ask, "Why Grails? Why another framework?" That was my thought when I first heard about Grails.

I was at a conference that featured sessions on an array of Java-related technologies and was planning to attend several talks on JavaServer Faces (JSF), which is what I was working with at the time. During one of the time slots where there was nothing JSF-related, I wandered into a session on Grails by Scott Davis. And I have to say, I was impressed. But not convinced.

In the past, I had worked with so-called rapid application development tools on the desktop and had seen the trade-off that you had to make to get these "applications in minutes." As soon as you needed to do more than the tool was designed for, you were stuck. I didn't want to go down that road again. Still, Grails did look like it would be a good choice for *small* applications. So, I gave it a try.

After using Grails to build a website for our local Java user group, I was hooked. By day, I was struggling with JSF and Enterprise JavaBeans (EJB); by night, I was having a blast building a website with Grails. I began to look for ways to take advantage of the brilliant simplicity of Grails in my day job. After all, I worked in a Java shop, and Grails is a fully compliant JEE[1] framework. It would produce a standard .war file, which could be deployed on our commercial JEE application server. Finally, an opportunity presented itself.

It was a small but important public-facing web application, planned as a six-week JSF/EJB project. With Grails, it was done in three weeks—and it turned out to be a little less trivial than we thought, because we needed to integrate with an existing EJB server. We found that the Grails "magic" was great for most of the application and provided significant productivity boosts. We also found that when we needed to do something Grails didn't handle "out of the box,"[2] it was easy to dip into the underlying technologies and do what we needed. There were no black boxes or brick walls. It wasn't "the Grails way or the highway."

We went on to use Grails to rescue another, much larger project that was in trouble, with similar results. Grails is definitely not *just* for small applications!

How Does Grails Do It?

Grails takes a set of successful frameworks, each of which has made its own strides toward addressing the complexity of building web applications, and makes them all simpler, easier to use, and ultimately more powerful.

Grails bundles Spring, Hibernate, SiteMesh, H2, Tomcat, and a host of other battle-hardened frameworks, and following the principle of "convention over configuration,"[3] it removes the complexity for most use cases. And it uses the dynamic Groovy programming language to magically give us easy access to the combined power of these tools.

Recall from my story that on the projects I was involved in, Grails was a replacement for both JSF and EJB. JSF, like Struts before it and JSP before

---

1.   Java Enterprise Edition.
2.   I use this term with some hesitation—see http://dave-klein.blogspot.com/2008/08/out-of-box.html.
3.   See http://en.wikipedia.org/wiki/Convention_over_Configuration.

that, is intended to address the web tier (the front end). EJB was the framework we were using to provide persistence, transactions, and various other services (the back end). Grails addresses the whole application, and more important, it allows *us* to address the whole application. Using the frameworks mentioned earlier, Grails gives us a complete, seamless MVC[4] framework that is really more of a web application platform than just another framework.

Why This Book?

The idea for this book came about while working on the projects I mentioned earlier. I had been working with Grails for a while, but four other developers were working with me, and we really could have used a book to help bring them up to speed quickly. They didn't need a reference book yet but something more than a collection of articles and blog posts (as helpful as those are).

As Grails' exposure and acceptance continues to grow and as more and more developers have their "wow!" moments, it will become even more important to have a resource to help them get started quickly. That's the goal of this quick-start guide. It is not intended to be a reference or the only Grails book on your shelf. In this book, we'll help you get started and become productive with Grails, but you will no doubt want to go beyond that. To help you dig deeper, we've included lists of books, websites, blogs, and other helpful resources from the Groovy/Grails community in Appendix 2, *Resources*, on page 181.

This book is, however, intended to be more than a cursory introduction. We will cover all the basics of Grails and a few advanced topics as well. When we have finished our time together here, you will understand Grails well enough to use it in real projects. In fact, you will have already used it in a real project, because that is what we are going to do together. More on that later.

Who Should Read This Book

This book is aimed at web developers looking for relief from the pain brought on by the complexity of modern web development. If you dream in XML and enjoy juggling multiple layers of abstraction at a time or if you are in a job where your pay is based on the number of lines of code you write, then Grails may not be for you. If, on the other hand, you are looking for a way to be more productive, a way to be able to focus on the heart of your applications instead of all the technological bureaucracy, then you're in the right place.

---

4. Model View Controller. See http://en.wikipedia.org/wiki/Model-view-controller.

We assume you have an understanding of web application development, but you don't need to be an expert to benefit from Grails and from this book. An understanding of Java or another object-oriented programming language would be helpful. If you have experience with Spring and Hibernate, you are ahead of the curve, but if you've never even heard of them, you'll do fine. You can go quite far with Grails and be using Spring and Hibernate extensively without even realizing it. Finally, the language of Grails is Groovy. We won't assume that you have any experience with Groovy, and you won't need a great deal of it to get going with Grails. However, some knowledge of Groovy syntax and constructs will be helpful, so we will start out with a brief tutorial.

Source Code

The code for the project in this book is available for download. You can find a link to the source code on the book's home page: http://pragprog.com/titles/dkgrails2. At the top of most code listings, there is a colored box that shows where this code can be found in the source code repository. In the ebook version of the book, this is a link directly to the code file. You'll notice that the path shown in these boxes is different from the one suggested in the text; this is because we have multiple snapshots of the project at different stages, one for each chapter.

Grails Versions

The examples in this book have been tested with Grails 2.3.1. For newer Grails versions, keep an eye on the *Grails: A Quick-Start Guide* blog (http://gquick.blogspot.com) for any potential breaking changes and workarounds.

Acknowledgments

First, and most of all, I thank my Creator and Savior, Jesus Christ. Without Him I could do nothing, and I know that every good thing I have comes from Him (James 1:17). I am also very grateful to the many individuals who helped bring this book about and/or make it better. This book has been a family project, but there wasn't room on the cover to put all of our names. My wonderful wife, Debbie, and our crew: Zachary, Abigail, Benjamin, Sarah, Solomon, Hannah, Joanna, Rebekah, Susanna, Noah, Samuel, Gideon, Joshua, and Daniel all helped in various ways from proofreading/editing to just cheering me up and keeping me going. Thank you, and I love you all very much.

The technical reviewers, beta readers, and others who provided feedback for the first and second editions have made this book much better than I ever could have done on my own. Aitor Alzola, Jeff Brown, Doug Burns, Frederick Daoud, Scott Davis, Paolo Foletto, Amer Ghumrawi, Bill Gloff, Brian Grant,

Steve Harris, Brian Hogan, Dmitriy Kopylenko, Guillaume Laforge, Shih-gian Lee, John Penrod, Jared Richardson, Nathaniel Schutta, Ken Sipe, Dan Sline, Matt Stine, Venkat Subramaniam, Michael Easter, Ray Tayek, Vick Dini, Jeff Holland, and Andy Keffalas: thank you all so much for your help and encouragement!

Writing a book for the Pragmatic Programmers has been an awesome experience, and I am very grateful to them for giving me this opportunity. Dave, Andy, Colleen, Jackie, and Susannah: working with you has been an honor, a privilege, and a lot of fun! I can't wait to do it again!

Many others helped bring this book about in various ways, though they may not know it. I'd like to thank the gang at the Culver's in Portage, Wisconsin, for their cheerful faces, for their free wireless, and for not chasing me out even after closing time. To the speakers on the No Fluff Just Stuff symposium tour and Jay Zimmerman, their ringleader: thank you for your inspiration, encouragement, and example! Matthew Porter, Craig McElroy, and the rest of the gang at Contegix: thank you for giving me the opportunity to spend some time at such an exciting company and for your continued support of the Grails community. I'd also like to thank my former co-worker (and the best programmer in the world) Nate Neff for attempting to temper my enthusiasm (it's not gonna work).

Finally, I'd like to thank the Grails development team and the Grails community for making web development so much fun.

Dave Klein
November 2013

CHAPTER 1

Enough Groovy to Be Dangerous

Groovy is a dynamic language for the Java Virtual Machine (JVM). Of all the JVM languages, Groovy has the best integration with Java and probably the lowest barrier to entry for Java developers. Java is considered by many to be in the "C family" of languages; that is to say that its syntax borrows heavily from the C language. Other languages in this family are C++, C#, and, by its close relationship to Java, Groovy. Without getting into a debate on whether that syntax family is a good one, we can say it is one that millions of developers are familiar with. That means that millions of developers can quickly pick up Groovy!

Groovy—like Spring, Hibernate, and the other frameworks used in Grails—is included in the Grails install. You do not need to install Groovy to use Grails. However, Groovy is a great multipurpose language, and we encourage you to download it and take it for a spin. You will quickly become more productive in areas like XML processing, database access, file manipulation, and more. You can download the Groovy installation and find more information on the Groovy website.[1] Some excellent books are available on Groovy such as *Programming Groovy 2: Dynamic Productivity for the Java Developer [Sub13]*, *Making Java Groovy [Kou13]*, and *Groovy In Action [Koe13]*.

We're going to discuss the Groovy features that are most often used in a Grails application. But first, for the benefit of Java developers, we'll look at some of the differences between Java and Groovy.

Groovy Syntax Compared to Java

Despite the overall syntactic similarities, there are some differences between Groovy and Java that are worth noting. The first thing you'll notice in a block

---

1. http://groovy.codehaus.org

of Groovy code is the lack of semicolons; in Groovy, semicolons are optional. Return statements are also optional. If there is no return statement in a method, then the last statement evaluated is returned. Sometimes this makes sense, especially in the case of small methods that simply return a value or perform a single calculation. Other times it can be confusing. That's the beauty of the word *optional*. When return makes code more readable, use it; when it doesn't, don't.

Parentheses for method calls are optional in most cases, the exception being when calling a method without any arguments. Here are some examples:

```
x = someMethodWithArgs arg1, arg2, arg3
y = someMethodWithoutArgs()
```

Methods without arguments need the parentheses so that Groovy can tell them apart from *properties*. Groovy provides "real" properties.[2] All fields in a Groovy class are given *getters* and *setters* at compile time. When you access a field of a Groovy class, it may look like you are directly accessing the field, but behind the scenes, the getter or setter is being called. If you're not convinced, you can call them explicitly. They'll be there even though you didn't code them.

introduction.2/get_property.groovy
```
class Person {
    String name
}
def person = new Person()
person.name = 'Abigail'
assert person.getName() == 'Abigail'
person.setName('Abi')
assert person.name == 'Abi'
```

If you *explicitly declare* a get or set method for a property, it will be used as expected.

introduction.2/explicit_set_property.groovy
```
class Person {
    String name

    void setName(String val){
        name = val.toUpperCase()
    }
}
def person = new Person(name:'Sarah')
assert person.name == 'SARAH'
```

---

2. Joe Nuxoll provides a good explanation of the concept of properties at http://web.archive.org/web/20080829124045/http://blogs.sun.com/joe/resource/java-properties-events.pdf.

The previous snippet shows a few other differences in Groovy. First, all Groovy classes automatically get a named-args constructor. This is a constructor that takes a Map and calls the set method for each key that corresponds to a property.[3] You can easily see how this might save several lines of code with larger classes. Grails takes advantage of this feature to assign the values from a web page to a new object instance. Second, in Groovy, types are optional. Instead of giving a variable an explicit type, we can use the def keyword to designate that this variable will be *dynamically* typed. The third difference is the use of == in the assert statements. In Groovy, == is the same as calling the equals() method on the left operand.

Now, the toUpperCase() method we just used is the same as in Java. But for a little fun, we can modify that last example to try one of the many methods that Groovy adds to the String class.[4]

introduction.2/reverse.groovy
```
class Person {
    String name

    void setName(String val){
        name = val.toUpperCase().reverse()
    }
}

Person p = new Person(name:'Hannah')

assert p.name == 'HANNAH'
```

It worked. (Trust us.)

Not only does Groovy enhance the java.lang.String class, but it also adds an entirely new one.

Groovy Strings

Groovy adds a new string known as a GString. A GString can be created by declaring a literal with double quotes; a string literal with single quotes is a java.lang.String. A GString can be used in place of a Java String. If a method is expecting a String and is given a GString, it will be cast at runtime.

The beauty and power of the GString is its ability to evaluate embedded Groovy expressions. Groovy expressions can be designated in two ways. For simple

---

3. Any elements in the map that do not correspond to a property are ignored by the named-args constructor.
4. You can find more goodies in the API docs at http://groovy.codehaus.org/groovy-jdk/java/lang/String.html.

values that are not directly adjacent to any plain text, you can just use a dollar sign, like this:

```
"Hello $name"
```

For more involved expressions, you can use the dollar sign and a pair of curly braces:

```
"The 5th letter in 'Encyclopedia' is ${'Encyclopedia'[4]}"
```

There can be any number of expressions in a given GString, and single quotes can be embedded without any escaping. This comes in handy when generating HTML, as we'll see later. For now, let's take a look at the GString in action.

introduction.2/hello_groovy_string.groovy

```
def name = 'Zachary'
def x = 3
def y = 7
def groovyString = "Hello ${name}, did you know that $x x $y equals ${x*y}?"
assert groovyString == 'Hello Zachary, did you know that 3 x 7 equals 21?'
```

Groovy Closures

A Groovy closure, in simple terms, is an executable block of code that can be assigned to a variable, passed to a method, and executed.[5] Many of the enhancements Groovy has made to the standard Java libraries involved adding methods that take a closure as a parameter.

A closure is declared by placing code between curly braces. It can be declared as it is being passed to a method call, or it can be assigned to a variable and used later. A closure can take parameters by listing them after the opening curly brace and separating them from the code with a *dash-rocket* (->), like so:

```
def c = {a, b ->  a + b}
```

If no parameters are declared in a closure, then one is implicitly provided: it's called it. Take a look at the following example:

introduction.2/closure_times.groovy

```
def name = 'Dave'
def c = {println "$name called this closure ${it+1} time${it > 0 ? 's' : ''}"}
assert c instanceof Closure
5.times(c)
```

---

5. There has been much discussion and some confusion over the definition of a "closure" in programming languages. Some argue that what Groovy defines as a closure isn't. If you're ever in town, we can discuss it over a cup of coffee, but for our purposes, we'll be referring to closures as defined at http://groovy.codehaus.org/Closures.

There's a fair bit of new stuff in these three lines of code. Let's start at the top. The variable name is available when the closure is executed. Anything that is in scope when the closure is created will be available when it is executed, even if it is being executed by code in a different class. This closure is being assigned to the variable c and has no declared parameters. It does have and use the implicit parameter it. The code in this closure takes advantage of another Groovy shortcut. What would be in Java System.out.println() is now just println(). When you look at the text of the GString that follows, it becomes obvious that this code will work only if whatever calls this closure passes it a single parameter that is a number. That's just what the times() method, which Groovy adds to Integer, does. The parentheses are not required for the times() method, but we added them to emphasize that the closure was being passed in as a parameter. The output from this code looks like this:

```
Dave called this closure 1 time
Dave called this closure 2 times
Dave called this closure 3 times
Dave called this closure 4 times
Dave called this closure 5 times
```

There is much more to the Groovy closure than we can cover here, and we highly recommend the coverage of this topic in Venkat Subramaniam's *Programming Groovy 2 [Sub13]*. We will see more examples of the closure in action as we look at Groovy collection classes.

Groovy Collections

Groovy offers many enhancements to the standard Java collection classes. We'll take a look at the three collection types that are most used in Grails. The List, Map, and Set are powerful tools, and Groovy gives them a new edge. We know—technically Map is not a collection; that is, it does not implement the Collection interface. But for our purposes, it is a *collection* in that it holds objects. So, leaving semantic sensitivities aside, let's look at what Groovy has done for these classes.

List

One of the first interesting things to learn about the List in Groovy is that it can be created with a literal declaration.

```
introduction.2/groovy_list.groovy
def colors = ['Red', 'Green', 'Blue', 'Yellow']
def empty = []
assert colors instanceof List
assert empty instanceof List
assert empty.class.name == 'java.util.ArrayList'
```

A comma-separated list inside square brackets is an initialized List. It can contain literal numbers, strings, or any other objects. This is a good time to point out that in Groovy, *everything* is an object. Even simple data types such as int or boolean are autoboxed objects. (That's why we were able to call the times() method on the literal 5 in our earlier example.) The last line of this example shows that the default List implementation in Groovy is java.util.ArrayList.

Groovy has also added a host of helpful methods to the List interface. One of the most useful is each(). This method is actually added to all objects in Groovy, but it is most useful with collection types. The each() method on List takes a closure as a parameter and calls that closure for each element in the List, passing in the element as the single it parameter.

introduction.2/groovy_list.groovy
```
def names = ['Nate', 'Matthew', 'Craig', 'Amanda']

names.each{
  println "The name $it contains ${it.size()} characters."
}
```

This example will print the following output to the console:

```
The name Nate contains 4 characters.
The name Matthew contains 7 characters.
The name Craig contains 5 characters.
The name Amanda contains 6 characters.
```

Two handy methods added by Groovy are min() and max():

introduction.2/groovy_list.groovy
```
assert names.min() == 'Amanda'
assert names.max() == 'Nate'
```

Groovy also provides a few easy ways to sort a List. The simple sort() method will provide a natural sort of the elements in the List. It can also take a closure. If the closure has no explicit parameters, then the implied it parameter can be used in an expression to sort on. You can also give the closure two parameters to represent two List elements, and then use those parameters in a comparison expression. Here are some examples:

introduction.2/groovy_list.groovy
```
def sortedNames = names.sort()
assert sortedNames == ['Amanda','Craig','Matthew','Nate']
sortedNames = names.sort{it.size()}
assert sortedNames == ['Nate','Craig','Amanda','Matthew']
sortedNames = names.sort{obj1, obj2 ->
  obj1[2] <=> obj2[2]
}
assert sortedNames == ['Craig','Amanda','Nate','Matthew']
```

The first example performs a natural sort on the names. The second example uses a closure to sort the names based on their size(). The last example, though admittedly contrived, is the more interesting one. In that example, we pass a closure to the sort(). This closure takes two parameters that represent two objects to be compared. In the body of the closure, we use the comparison operator[6] to compare some aspect of the two objects; in this case—and this is the contrived part—we compare the third character in the name with [2]. This type of sort would make more sense when the List elements are a more complex type and you need to sort on a combination of properties or a more complex expression, but you get the point.

Another useful feature of List is that the left shift operator (<<) can be used in place of the add() method:

introduction.2/groovy_list.groovy
```
names << 'Jim'
assert names.contains('Jim')
```

Map

The Map class contains a collection of key/value pairs. It also can be created with a literal declaration, like so:

introduction.2/groovy_map.groovy
```
def family = [boys:7, girls:6, Debbie:1, Dave:1]
def empty = [:]

assert family instanceof Map
assert empty instanceof Map
assert empty.getClass().name == 'java.util.LinkedHashMap'
```

The Map class in Groovy also has the each() method. When it is given a closure without any parameters, the implicit it will be a Map.Entry containing key and value properties. The more common approach is to give the closure two parameters: the first parameter will hold the key, and the second parameter will hold the value.

introduction.2/groovy_map.groovy
```
def favoriteColors = [Ben:'Green',Solomon:'Blue',Joanna:'Red']
favoriteColors.each{key, value ->
    println "${key}'s favorite color is ${value}."
}
```

The output from this code would be as follows:

---

6. <=> is a shortcut for the compareTo() method.

```
Ben's favorite color is Green.
Solomon's favorite color is Blue.
Joanna's favorite color is Red.
```

In Groovy, Map entries can be accessed using dot notation, as if they were properties. You may have noticed that in our first Map example, we had to use empty.getClass().name instead of the Groovy shortcut empty.class.name. That's because empty.class would have looked for a key in empty called class. Other than a few edge cases like that, this is the preferred way to access Map values.

introduction.2/groovy_map.groovy
```
assert favoriteColors.Joanna == 'Red'
```

There is no overridden left shift operator for Map, but adding an element is still a snap. Assigning a value to a key that doesn't exist will add that key and value to the Map.

introduction.2/groovy_map.groovy
```
favoriteColors.Rebekah = 'Pink'
assert favoriteColors.size() == 4
assert favoriteColors.containsKey('Rebekah')
```

Set

The Set class also implements the Collection interface, so most of what we saw with List applies to it as well. Set is the default type for one-to-many associations in Grails, so we'll be working with it often. There are a couple of notable differences between Set and List. First, a Set can't contain duplicates, and second, it can't be accessed with the subscript operator ([]). This last difference can be a hindrance, but it is easy to overcome with the toList() method.

introduction.2/groovy_set.groovy
```
def employees = ['Susannah','Noah','Samuel','Gideon'] as Set
Set empty = []

assert employees instanceof Set
assert empty instanceof Set
assert empty.class.name == 'java.util.HashSet'

employees << 'Joshua'

assert employees.contains('Joshua')

println employees.toList()[4]
```

In this example, we create a Set with four names in it. Since we didn't declare employees with a type, we need to cast it as a Set. (The default type for a literal declaration like this is ArrayList.) We could have just declared the type explicitly, as we do with empty on the next line. Then we add another item to the Set using the handy left shift operator and assert() that it is there. Finally, we show that there are now five items by printing the fifth one with println employees.toList()[4]. This is the output from the last line of that example: Samuel. This brings up another point about Set: you have no control of the order in which elements are stored. If you need to specify an order, either sorted or creation order, you can use a SortedSet or List.

Many more methods are added to these classes that we don't have space to cover here. To become more productive in Groovy (and to have more "wow!" moments), check out the Groovy JDK docs, at http://groovy.codehaus.org/groovy-jdk.

Metaprogramming

A complete discussion of Groovy's metaprogramming features would be beyond the scope of this primer, but it will be helpful to have some understanding of them as you begin to work with Grails. Groovy's metaprogramming can make us much more productive as developers. With it, Grails adds methods to our objects that we are going to *need* and *use* but never *write*.

So here's Groovy metaprogramming in a nutshell: Groovy provides mechanisms for adding methods and properties to classes at runtime, and/or without touching their code. This is done in several ways; we'll discuss two that are used in Grails.

Every Groovy class has a metaClass, which can be written by someone else and assigned at runtime. Any methods or properties added in a class's metaClass will also be available in that class, and the behavior of a class can be changed dynamically by assigning a different metaClass to it.

Groovy classes can also implement a method called methodMissing(). This is called when a method is called that does not exist in a class or its metaClass—the called method, along with any arguments, are passed to methodMissing(). So, for example, we could add a methodMissing() to the metaClass of Integer, and have it look for the string incrementBy in the called method. If the rest of the method name converts to a number, our methodMissing could add that to the current value. Then we could do something crazy like:

```
25.incrementBy5()
```

As we'll begin to see in *Creating a Domain Class*, on page 21, when we create a domain class in Grails, it will have methods, such as save(), that we didn't have to implement. At first it may seem like magic, but it's really just Groovy metaprogramming at work. And it sure does a lot of work for us!

For a much more thorough explanation of metaprogramming and examples of how to use this powerful tool in your own applications, take a look at *Programming Groovy 2 [Sub13]* by Venkat Subramaniam.

Where to from Here?

Now that you have some Groovy basics under your belt, we're ready to get into Grails. Over the next 11 chapters, we'll be exploring most areas of the Grails framework. We won't spend a great deal of time on any one feature, and we may not cover every aspect of Grails. The goal is to give you the knowledge and experience necessary to start working effectively and productively with Grails and to point you to the resources you'll need as you continue.

"Experience?" you say. "How do I get experience from a book?" This book is meant not only to be read but to be *used.* In this Groovy tutorial, we showed some code snippets and explained them. In the rest of the book, we'll be working together on a real project. By the time you finish this book, you'll have developed and deployed your first full-featured web application with Grails.

Finally, an appendix at the end of the book contains resources (websites, blogs, books, and mailing lists) available in the thriving Groovy and Grails community.

Let's get started!

Tell me and I forget. Teach me and I remember.
Involve me and I learn.

  ➤ *Benjamin Franklin*

CHAPTER 2

Our Project

When you're learning a new tool or language, you might start with a "Hello World" example or perhaps work through a few exercises in a book. Those steps can help you become acquainted with the tool, but that's as far as they'll take you. If you want to become productive in a tool or even proficient, you need use it in a real project. So, that's what we're going to do. We'll work together to build a cool new web application—one that will actually go live. As our application comes together, we'll explore Grails in a thorough, practical way. This strategy will provide us with the context that is so valuable in understanding and becoming productive with a new framework.

We'll be working through a series of iterations, covering about one iteration per chapter. This means that some features of Grails will be used in more than one chapter. We want to build a real application, and the repetition that comes with that is a good thing. This is a quick-start guide, but we don't want it to be a false-start guide. When our time together is over, you'll be able to go on to your second Grails project with confidence.

One concern with this method of discovery is that we're going to run into more advanced features of Grails, perhaps before we are ready. We'll handle this potential problem by developing our application in an incremental manner. In other words, our application will start simple, thereby exercising the simple features in Grails, and gradually get more complex.

Introducing TekDays.com

The decision about what kind of project to take on in our quest to learn Grails is an important one. We want something that is substantial enough to exercise the framework in ways that will stick in our minds but not something that is so daunting that we are unable to finish it. We're also aiming for something useful *and* interesting. After all, you may need something more than our charm and wit to keep your attention.

Here's an issue many developers encounter: the rapid pace of technological innovation today is making it more difficult and, at the same time, increasingly important to keep our skills as developers up-to-date. One great way to keep on top of innovations and advances is to attend technical conferences, but with tightening training budgets at many companies and more developers working as freelancers or independent contractors, it is often hard to afford these events. Some developers have taken to organizing local, nonprofit mini-conferences to help address the problem. You may have heard of these events, such as the Houston Tech Fest, Silicon Valley Code Camp, or the bar camps that are springing up all over.[1] Wouldn't it be great if there was an online application to help individuals connect and put on these types of events? Well, when we're done here, there will be!

TekDays.com is going to be a site where people can announce, plan, and promote local, grassroots technical conferences. It will all start when visionary individuals suggest an event in their city. Then, as others hear about it and register their interest and/or support, we'll provide tools to help them organize the event: a to-do list, an organizer's dashboard (to keep track of volunteers, sponsors, and potential attendees), a discussion forum, and, finally, an event home page to help with promotion. This may sound like a tall order, but Grails can make it happen.

Meet Our Customer

One of the major benefits of Grails is its ability to provide rapid feedback. In minutes, we can have new features up and running and ready for our customers to try. But that benefit is hard to realize if we don't have a customer around. And this application is about building community: making connections, sharing ideas, and working together to build a solution. This application is going to production; in fact, we're going to use it to organize a real tech conference, so your authors, Dave and Ben, will be joining you on the dev team as well as playing the role of on-site customer—*and* first end user. Don't worry; we have experience wearing multiple hats. As we work on TekDays, you can show us what you've done, and we'll let you know what we think about it. Fair enough?

---

1. For more information on these events, see http://www.houstontechfest.org, http://www.siliconvalley-codecamp.com, and http://en.wikipedia.org/wiki/BarCamp.

Application Requirements

As your *customer*, we want to give you a good idea of what we are looking for in this application. We are trying to attract conference organizers to this site —preferably many of them. We're convinced of the value of these types of conferences to individual developers, communities, and the industry as a whole. The application should make it easy for those visionary individuals to get started by simply proposing a conference. Then it has to provide real help in bringing their vision to fruition.

As *end users*, we're hoping to use this application to organize a technical conference in St. Louis, Missouri. This is a big undertaking, and we know that we can't do it alone, so we need this application to make it easy for others to volunteer, or to at least let us know they're interested in attending. Some type of workflow to guide us through the process would make this whole endeavor much less daunting.

After this introduction and a follow-up discussion with our customer and user, we've come up with the following feature list for our application:

- Create new events
- Display event details
- Edit event details
- Create users/organizers
- Allow users to volunteer to help
- Add users to events
- Allow anonymous users to register interest
- Create sponsors
- Add sponsors to events
- Have default list of tasks
- Add/remove tasks
- Assign tasks to users
- Post forum message
- Reply to forum message
- Display forum message threads
- Allow access to event home page with simple URL

This list gives us a good idea of the scope of the project. When we're done here, people will be able to propose conferences, volunteer to help, or add their support. Organizers will be able to assign tasks to volunteers to spread the load, and questions can be asked and answered in the forums to keep the communication flowing. As a conference begins to take shape, we'll provide the tools needed to promote it successfully. Businesses will be able to bring their resources to bear to help make it all happen. This is getting exciting!

We will, of course, need to flesh these out more as we go along. During each iteration, we'll design and implement two or three features. Along the way, we (or our customer) may come up with new features or changes. That's OK. Grails can handle it, and so can we.

Iteration Zero

Before we get started building our application, we'll take a few moments to set the stage.

Installing Grails

First off, let's get Grails installed and set up. There are a few different ways to install Grails, with installers on one end of the spectrum and building the source from GitHub on the other. We'll use that happy middle ground and download the compressed binaries. They are at http://grails.org/download and are made available as zip files. Once we have them, follow these steps:

1. Expand the archive to a directory on your computer.
2. Set your GRAILS_HOME environment variable to this directory.
3. Add GRAILS_HOME/bin to your path.
4. Ensure that you have a JAVA_HOME environment variable pointing to a JDK version 1.6 or higher.

To test our installation, run the following command:

```
$ grails help
```

If this returns something like the following output, then we're good to go:

```
| Environment set to development.....

Usage (optionals marked with *):
grails [environment]* [options]* [target] [arguments]*

Examples:
grails dev run-app
grails create-app books
```

```
Available options:
 -debug-fork                    Whether to debug the forked JVM if using
                                forked mode
 -verbose                       Enable verbose output
 -plain-output                  Disables ANSI output
 -refresh-dependencies          Whether to force a resolve of dependencies
                                (skipping any caching)
 -reloading                     Enable the reloading agent
 -stacktrace                    Enable stack traces in output
 -offline                       Indicates that Grails should not connect
                                to any remote servers during processing of
                                the build
 -version                       Current Grails version
 -non-interactive               Whether to allow the command line to
                                request input

Available Targets (type grails help 'target-name' for more info):
grails add-proxy
grails alias
grails bootstrap
grails bug-report
grails clean
...
```

If you don't see this output, verify that your GRAILS_HOME and JAVA_HOME environment variables are valid and that GRAILS_HOME/bin is on your path. You can do this easily with echo:

```
$ echo $GRAILS_HOME
$ echo $JAVA_HOME
$ echo $PATH
```

On Windows, this would be as follows:

```
> echo %GRAILS_HOME%
> echo %JAVA_HOME%
> echo %PATH%
```

Grails Scripts

Grails comes with more than seventy built-in scripts that can be run with the grails command. These scripts are used for creating applications and application artifacts, as well as to run tests or to run the application. We'll learn about many of these as we work on TekDays. If you want to explore the others, you can do that with grails help. As we saw in the previous section, grails help will show you a list of the scripts that come with the framework. To find out more about any one of them, run grails help followed by the name of the script. For example:

```
$ grails help run-app
```

Although we will be using the built-in scripts only to get TekDays ready for production, it's worth noting that other scripts can be used with the grails command; some plugins install new scripts, and it's also possible to write your own scripts for Grails.

Setting Up Our Workspace

In other web frameworks that we've used—especially Java-based frameworks —starting a new project is an ordeal. If you're lucky, there might be a wizard, or perhaps there's a template project you can copy and customize. Even with those aids, getting everything set up and in the right place can be a drag. Grails has a solution to this problem, in the form of a script called create-app. We'll use this script to get TekDays off the ground.

From the directory that will be the parent of our project directory, enter the following command:

```
$ grails create-app TekDays
```

When we run the command, Grails creates a bunch of directories and files for our project. In just a bit, we'll take a closer look at the directories that are created and what they are used for.

The TekDays project is now ready to go. In fact, we can even run it already:

```
$ cd TekDays
$ grails run-app
```

Here's a summarized view of the output from the run-app script:

```
| Loading Grails 2.3.1
| Configuring classpath
| Environment set to development.....
| Running Grails application
| Server running. Browse to http://localhost:8080/TekDays
```

Early on in the output, Grails tells us that the environment is set to development. development is the default of the three standard Grails environments. Running in the development environment (or in development mode, as it is often called) gives us autoreloading (we can change most aspects of the application while it's running and see the changes immediately) and an in-memory database to make that rapid feedback even more rapid. These types of productivity-enhancing features can be added to most other frameworks via external tools and libraries, but Grails bakes them right in. The other two environments are test and production. We'll return to these other environments later when we get to testing and deployment. For now, keep in mind that these are only defaults and can be changed if needed.

The last line of output tells us where to go to see our application in action. In the following figure, we can see what we get by browsing to that location.

Figure 1—We start with a working application.

The default home page of the app displays some application statistics in the sidebar, as well as a list of installed plugins and a list of the app's controllers. (There is only one controller to begin with: grails.plugin.databasemigration.DbdocController is part of the Grails Database Migration plugin,[2] which is automatically installed by Grails.)

It may not look like much yet, but having a working application from the very beginning is just *powerful.* It gives us an excellent feedback loop. We'll be maintaining that runnable state, and, consequently, that feedback loop, right through to deployment.

Starting with All Windows Intact

In their book *The Pragmatic Programmer [HT00],* Dave Thomas and Andy Hunt discuss the "Broken Window" theory as it relates to software development. This theory holds that if a building has a broken window that is left unrepaired, its chances of further vandalism are increased. Dave and Andy point out that if software is left in a partially broken state (failing tests or ignored bugs), it will continue to degenerate.

With many development tools and frameworks, we start out with broken windows; nothing works until multiple pieces are in place. This makes it easier to get started and keep coding without taking the time to see whether what we have *works.* With Grails we start out with a running application; as we make changes, we get immediate feedback that lets us know whether we've broken something.

---

2. See http://grails.org/plugin/database-migration.

With some other web frameworks, we would have had to create one or two source files, an index page, and a handful of XML files to get this far. All it took in Grails was a single command.

Anatomy of a Grails Project

Now that we've seen our application run, let's take a look at what's under the hood. When we ran the create-app script, a number of files and directories were generated for us. (See the next figure.) The files that were created have default code and configuration information that we can change as needed. The directories are particularly important because they are at the heart of Grails' "convention over configuration" strategy. Each directory has a purpose, and when files are placed in these directories and meet certain other conventions, *magical things* will happen. We will look at most of these in more detail when we begin to work with them. For now, here's a brief overview:

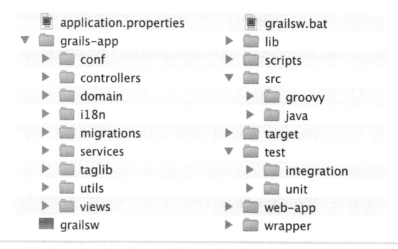

Figure 2—The files and directories of a Grails application

- grails-app: The main application directory, which contains the following directories:

  - conf: Contains Grails configuration files and directories for optional Hibernate and Spring configuration files[3]

  - controllers: Holds the controller classes, the entry points into a Grails application

  - domain: Holds domain classes, representing persistent data

---

3. Most Grails applications will not need Spring or Hibernate configuration files.

- i18n: Holds message property files for internationalization

- migrations: Can contain change log files generated by the Grails Database Migration plugin

- services: Holds service classes, which are Spring-managed beans

- taglib: Holds Groovy Server Pages (GSP) custom tag libraries

- utils: Holds codec classes[4]

- views: Holds the GSP views

- lib: Contains any external .jar files we may need to include (such as JDBC drivers).

- scripts: Can contain custom Groovy scripts to be used in the application.

- src: Contains directories for other Java and Groovy source files. Files in this directory are available to the application at runtime.

- target: Created when we first run the app. It contains artifacts produced by Grails commands such as grails war.

- test: Contains directories for unit and integration tests.

- web-app: Contains directories for images, CSS, and JavaScript.

- wrapper: Can contain wrapper files generated by the wrapper script.

The application.properties file holds our application's name and version, along with a list of plugins used. The default version for a new Grails application is 0.1; we can change this in application.properties. The grailsw shell script and grailsw.bat batch file allow our project to be run without a manual installation of Grails; if Grails isn't installed when they're run, they will download it and set it up to work with our project, and can then be used to run Grails scripts in place of the usual grails command.

A brief word about tools: support for Groovy and Grails in most of the popular development tools is good and getting better all the time. Integrated development environments (IDEs) such as Eclipse, NetBeans, and IntelliJ IDEA are a big help in managing a multitude of configuration files or for dealing with verbose and redundant language syntax, but with Grails' use of "convention over configuration" and the clean, concise syntax of Groovy, we find ourselves turning to an IDE less and less. If you really feel the need for an IDE, you can find more information about what's available in Appendix 2, *Resources*, on

---

4. See http://grails.org/doc/2.3.1/guide/single.html#codecs.

page 181. As we work on TekDays, we'll be using the command line for interacting with Grails, but coding can be done in an editor or IDE.

Summary

We're off to a good start. We have Grails installed. Our project requirements are clear and achievable. Our new application is prepped, ready, and running.

In the next chapter, we'll begin our first development iteration. To get ourselves acclimated, we'll reach for some low-hanging fruit and work on the first three features on our list. At the end of Chapter 3, we will be able to create, display, and edit an event.

Laying the Foundation

In this chapter, we'll implement the first three features on the TekDays feature list. We'll add the ability to create, view, and modify new technical conferences (or code camps or what have you). We will refer to all of these as *events*. These events are the core of our application. Each event that is created here has the potential to become an actual gathering of dozens, if not hundreds, of developers, designers, architects, and maybe even project managers, all learning, sharing, and generally advancing our craft.

The three features that we'll be implementing are very closely related; they're so close, in fact, that we will be implementing them all at once! Grails dynamically adds the ability to create, read, update, and delete data from a *domain class*. We will take advantage of this to get us started, but we won't stop there.

Creating a Domain Class

The heart of a Grails application is its *domain model*, that is, the set of domain classes and their relationships.

A domain class represents *persistent data* and, by default, is used to create a table in a database. We'll talk more about this shortly when we create our first domain class. For creating domain classes, Grails provides a convenience script called (unsurprisingly)[1] create-domain-class.

Just as the domain model is the heart of a Grails application, the TekEvent class will be the heart of the TekDays domain model. TekEvent is the name of the class that we will use to represent an event (or conference or code camp or tech fest). If we were to sit down and put our heads together to come up

---

1. The designers of Grails followed the *principle of least surprise*; most names in Grails are common sense and therefore easy to remember.

with a design for the TekEvent class, we'd probably end up with something similar to what we see in the following figure.

Figure 3—Diagram of the TekEvent class

To create our TekEvent class, run the following command:

```
$ grails create-domain-class com.tekdays.TekEvent
```

This script expects a package; we're using the package com.tekdays. If we didn't give it a package, the script would default to the name of the app, so our classes would be in the tekdays package.

The output from this command has a few lines of introductory text and then these two lines:

```
| Created file grails-app/domain/com/tekdays/TekEvent.groovy
| Created file test/unit/com/tekdays/TekEventSpec.groovy
```

Grails created two files for us: the domain class and a unit test class (specifically, a Spock specification).[2] This is an example of the way that Grails makes it easier for us to do the right thing. We still need to add tests, but having this test class already created for us gives us a little nudge in the right direction.

In Grails, a domain class is a Groovy class located under grails-app/domain. Let's take a look:

```
package com.tekdays

class TekEvent {

    static constraints = {
    }
}
```

---

2. Spock (https://code.google.com/p/spock/) is a specification testing framework for Groovy and Java applications. We'll discuss Grails' generated Spock tests in *Testing Our Domain Class*, on page 24.

Pretty anemic, huh? Grails is powerful, but it's not omniscient. (Maybe in the next release....) We have to write a little code to make our TekEvent class useful. We'll use Groovy properties (see *Groovy Syntax Compared to Java*, on page 1) to flesh out our domain class. It's time to fire up your trusty editor and add the following properties to the TekEvent class:

foundation.2/TekDays/grails-app/domain/com/tekdays/TekEvent.groovy
```
String city
String name
String organizer
String venue
Date startDate
Date endDate
String description
```

We will need to come back to this class later and add or change things. Notice that we gave our organizer property a type of String, but our diagram shows a User. That's because we don't have a User class yet. A look at our feature list shows us we will need one. But don't worry: refactoring a Grails application, especially in the early stages, is a breeze.

While you have your editor out, why not add a toString() method to TekEvent too? This always comes in handy, since it gives us an easy way to represent an instance of our domain class as a String. We'll see later that Grails takes advantage of the toString() in the views that it generates, and if we don't create our own, we'll get Grails' default, which is not all that informative or user friendly.

Groovy makes this very easy to do. Add the following code after the properties we just added:

foundation.2/TekDays/grails-app/domain/com/tekdays/TekEvent.groovy
```
String toString(){
  "$name, $city"
}
```

This toString() method will return the name and city of the TekEvent separated by a comma. For a refresher on what's going on here, take another look at *Groovy Syntax Compared to Java*, on page 1 and *Groovy Strings*, on page 3.

More About Domain Classes

Now we have a persistent TekEvent class. We can create instances of this class and save them to the database. We can even find existing instances by their id or by their properties. You might be wondering how that can be—where is the code for all this functionality? We'll learn more about that when we start

Joe asks:

If Groovy Is a Dynamic Language, Why Are We Specifying the Types of Our Properties?

That's an excellent question. If you were creating a persistent class, why might you want to have data types on the properties? If your answer had something to do with the database schema, move to the head of the class! Groovy *is* a dynamic language, and our properties *could* be declared with the def keyword rather than a type, but by using types, Grails is able to tell our database what data type to use when defining columns. Grails also uses type information to choose default HTML elements for our views.

using these features, but the short answer is that Grails uses Groovy metaprogramming (which we discussed in *Metaprogramming*, on page 9) to dynamically add powerful behavior to our domain classes. As we get further in developing our application, we'll see that we can call methods like TekEvent.save(), TekEvent.list(), and TekEvent.findAllByStartDateGreaterThan(new Date() - 30), even though we've never written any code to implement those methods.

Because domain classes are such an integral part of a Grails application, we will be coming back to them frequently as we work on TekDays, learning a bit more each time. There is, however, one more feature we should discuss before we continue. Along with dynamically adding several methods and nonpersistent properties to our domain classes, Grails adds two persistent properties: id and version. These properties are both Integers. The id property is the unique key in the table that is created, and the version is used by Grails for *optimistic concurrency*.[3]

Testing Our Domain Class

As mentioned earlier, Grails makes it easy for us to do the right thing by generating test classes for us, but we still have to write the tests. So, let's add a test for our TekEvent class.

Grails includes the JUnit testing framework wrapped in Groovy goodness, along with the Spock specification framework. When we created our domain class, a Spock test class was created for us in the test/unit directory.

---

3. Optimistic concurrency is a way of keeping a user's changes from getting stomped on by another user changing the same data at the same time. It's outside the scope of this book, but see http://en.wikipedia.org/wiki/Optimistic_concurrency_control for more information.

By default Grails provides two types of testing, *unit* and *integration*.[4] (The test Grails generated for TekEvent is, of course, a unit test.) Since the goal of a unit test is to test a single class in isolation, Grails unit tests do not provide access to any of the dynamic behavior that would otherwise be available.

Testing and Dynamic Languages

Writing automated tests for our code is always a good idea, but it becomes even more important when working with a dynamic language such as Groovy. In some situations, it's possible for a simple typo that would be caught by the Java compiler to sneak through and cause havoc at runtime. Automated unit tests can prevent that and much more. A compiler will verify that our code is syntactically correct, but a well-written test will verify that it works! As Stuart Halloway once said, "In five years, we will view compilation as a really weak form of unit testing."

Fortunately, writing unit tests in Groovy is *much* easier than it would be in a language such as Java or C#. See Chapter 19, "Unit Testing and Mocking," in *Programming Groovy 2 [Sub13]* for more information on applying the power of Groovy to unit testing.

At this point, most of the functionality of the TekEvent class is dynamic. However, we can write a test for the toString() method. Open TekDays/test/unit/com/tekdays/TekEventSpec.groovy. You should see something like this:

```
package com.tekdays

import grails.test.mixin.TestFor
import spock.lang.Specification

/**
 * See the API for {@link grails.test.mixin.domain.DomainClassUnitTestMixin}
 * for usage instructions
 */
@TestFor(TekEvent)
class TekEventSpec extends Specification {

    def setup() {
    }

    def cleanup() {
    }

    void "test something"() {
    }
}
```

---

4. We'll learn more about integration tests in *Integration Testing*, on page 98.

Grails uses the TestFor annotation to indicate the class that's being tested. In the generated test class here, we have one stubbed-out test called "test something"(). We can add as many tests as we want to a Grails test class. We are currently adding only one test, so we will just replace "test something"() with a "test toString"() method. Modify the test class to look like this:

foundation.2/TekDays/test/unit/com/tekdays/TekEventSpec.groovy
```groovy
package com.tekdays

import grails.test.mixin.TestFor
import spock.lang.Specification

/**
 * See the API for {@link grails.test.mixin.domain.DomainClassUnitTestMixin}
 * for usage instructions
 */
@TestFor(TekEvent)
class TekEventSpec extends Specification {

    def setup() {
    }

    def cleanup() {
    }

    void "test toString"() {
        when: "a tekEvent has a name and a city"
                def tekEvent = new TekEvent(name:'Groovy One',
                                            city: 'San Francisco',
                                            organizer: 'John Doe')

        then: "the toString method will combine them."
                tekEvent.toString() == 'Groovy One, San Francisco'
    }
}
```

Our test code is simple enough. We are creating a new TekEvent, assigning it to the variable tekEvent, and stating that the return value of tekEvent.toString() is equal to the expected value.

Grails provides a script called test-app that will, by default, run all of our application's unit and integration tests. We can use the unit: flag to tell it to run only unit tests. This is helpful since we want to run our tests frequently and unit tests are much faster than integration tests. We can also specify the particular tests we want to run; test-app unit: TekEvent (note that we can omit the "Spec" suffix) will run only the unit tests for TekEvent. Let's use this now to run our test:

```
$ grails test-app unit: TekEvent
```

The output from this command ends with the following lines:

```
| Completed 1 unit test, 0 failed in 0m 1s
| Tests PASSED - view reports in .../TekDays/target/test-reports
```

The total number of tests run is shown, along with how many tests failed. (In our case, we have only one test, and it passed.) Then the result of the test-app command is shown. The result will be either Tests PASSED or Tests FAILED. Tests FAILED means that the tests ran with one or more assertion failures. In the event of a test failure, you will find very helpful information in the HTML reports that Grails produces. The final line of output from test-app gives the location of these reports.

As we create more artifacts throughout the course of the project, be sure to add valid tests for them. Otherwise when we run test-app, our test suite will fail, and kittens will die.

Taking Control of Our Domain

The next step in implementing our first features is to give our users a way to create TekEvent instances. To do this, we will need a *controller* class. Controller classes are the dispatchers of a Grails application. All requests from the browser come through a controller. We will do quite a bit of work with controller classes later, but for now all we need is a blank one. Once again, Grails has a script to produce this:

```
$ grails create-controller com.tekdays.TekEvent
```

This will create the files grails-app/controllers/com/tekdays/TekEventController.groovy and test/unit/com/tekdays/TekEventControllerSpec.groovy,[5] along with a folder for views (this folder will be empty to begin with). Let's open the TekEventController in our editor and take a look:

```
package com.tekdays

class TekEventController {

    def index() { }
}
```

The line that we see in this otherwise empty controller—def index() { }—is called an *action*. Specifically, the index action. We will eventually have controllers

---

5. We won't be working with the test file yet since we currently have virtually no code to test.

full of actions, but for now we will take advantage of a powerful Grails feature called *dynamic scaffolding*. Dynamic scaffolding will generate a controller with a set of actions and corresponding views (pages), which we will discuss shortly. To get all this magic, let's change the TekEventController to look like this:

```
foundation.2/TekDays/grails-app/controllers/com/tekdays/TekEventController.groovy
package com.tekdays

class TekEventController {

    def scaffold = TekEvent
}
```

Now when we run our application, we see a link titled com.tekdays.TekEventController on the index page. This link takes us to the *list* view. This is the first of four views that are made available by the dynamic scaffolding; the others are *create*, *edit*, and *show*. Run the application, navigate to http://localhost:8080/TekDays, and click that TekEventController link. You should see something like the following figure.

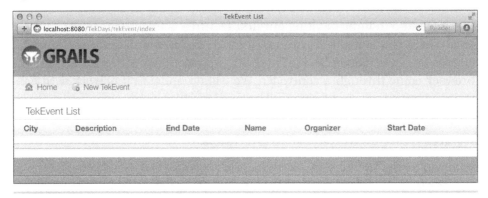

Figure 4—The scaffolded list view

The list is (obviously) empty, since we haven't created any events yet. In the menu bar of the list view, there is a button labeled "New TekEvent". This button will take us to the create view. (See Figure 5, *The scaffolded create view*, on page 29.) We'll have to tweak these views a bit, but first let's see what our customer thinks.

Modifying Code That Doesn't Exist

We put on our customer hat, and, after getting over our shock at how fast you got this much done, we found the following issues with these views:

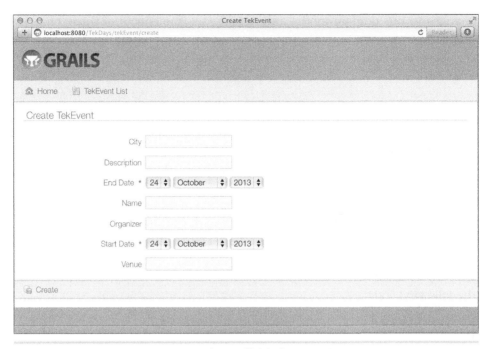

Figure 5—The scaffolded create view

- List view:

  - The Grails logo, while very cool, is not the logo we had in mind for TekDays.

  - What's with the order of the columns? We would prefer to see Name, City, Description, Organizer, Venue, and so on.

- Create view:

  - The logo and field order issues apply here too.

  - There is not enough room in the Description field to enter any meaningful content.

  - The date inputs allow for far too wide a range of years—we're not going to be putting on events in the year 1913.

Some of these issues will have to wait until we generate code that we can modify.[6] Currently we are using *dynamic scaffolding*, which allows us to make

---

6. Grails does provide a way to make more significant changes to dynamically scaffolded views with the install-templates script. You can read about it at http://grails.org/Artifact+and+Scaffolding+Templates.

changes to our domain model and quickly see the effects of those changes but doesn't provide us with any code that we can customize. However, we can fix some of the issues the customer brought up by modifying our TekEvent class.

Constraining Our Domain

Grails uses our domain classes to make some decisions about the scaffolding. For example, property types are used to determine which HTML elements to use. To go further, we can add *constraints* to our domain class. Constraints are a way of telling Grails more about the properties of our domain class. They are used for validation when saving, for determining some aspects of database schema generation, and for laying out scaffolded views. We'll look at those first two uses of constraints later (see *Constraints and Validation*, on page 54), but that last one is what we're going to take advantage of now. Open TekDays/grails-app/domain/com/tekdays/TekEvent.groovy in your trusty editor, and add the following code:

```
foundation.2/TekDays/grails-app/domain/com/tekdays/TekEvent.groovy
static constraints = {
    name()
    city()
    description maxSize: 5000
    organizer()
    venue()
    startDate()
    endDate()
}
```

The constraints consist of a code block, which is a Groovy closure.[7] Inside this block, we list each of our properties, followed by parentheses. For each property, we can include one or more key/value pairs that represent *constraints*—rules—for that property. (If we do assign constraints to a particular property, we can omit the parentheses.) The order of the properties in the constraints block will be used to determine the display order in the scaffolded views. The maxSize constraint that we added to the description property will affect how that property is displayed in the views and will also affect the database schema generation. For example, in MySQL,[8] the description field will be of type longtext, whereas nonconstrained String properties will render fields of varchar(255).

When we run the application and navigate to the list view, we see that it looks more like Figure 6, *List view with constraints*, on page 31.

---

7. See *Groovy Closures*, on page 4.
8. See http://dev.mysql.com.

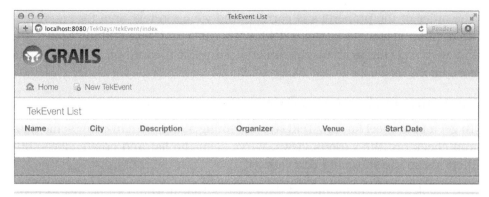

Figure 6—List view with constraints

In this view, we corrected only the order of the properties, but if we click the "New TekEvent" button, we see that the create page looks significantly better. (See the next figure.)

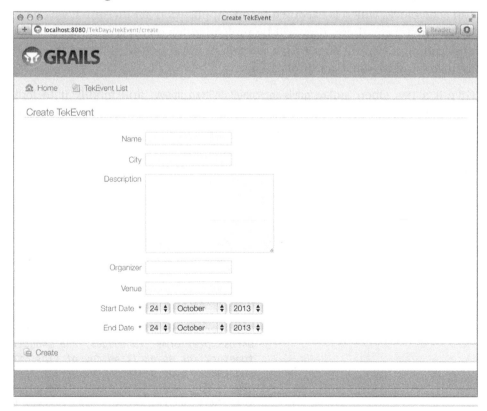

Figure 7—Create view with constraints

The order of the properties is correct, and we get a text area for entering a description instead of an input field. We haven't addressed all the issues yet, but we're moving in the right direction, and we'll continue to make small corrections as we go.

Bootstrapping Some Test Data

To get a better feel for how TekDays is coming along, we can enter some data and check out the various views. We've seen the list and create views, but there's also the show and edit views.

The problem with entering test data now is that it would all be lost as soon as we restarted the application. We're working with an *in-memory database* at this point. Eventually, we will point TekDays at a real database, but for now, the in-memory H2 database is pretty handy—that is, it would be if we didn't lose our data.

This dilemma's answer is in TekDays/grails-app/conf/BootStrap.groovy. The file has an init() code block, which is executed by our application at start-up. If we create TekEvent instances there, they will be preloaded for us every time we run the application. (Once we do set up a persistent database, we'll tweak this code to make sure we don't get duplicates.)

Give it a try. Open TekDays/grails-app/conf/BootStrap.groovy, and modify it to look similar to the following code. You can make up your own event. Be creative. It makes the learning process more fun.

```
foundation.2/TekDays/grails-app/conf/BootStrap.groovy
import com.tekdays.*

class BootStrap {

    def init = { servletContext ->
        def event1 = new TekEvent(name: 'Gateway Code Camp',
                    city: 'Saint Louis, MO',
                    organizer: 'John Doe',
                    venue: 'TBD',
                    startDate: new Date('11/21/2013'),
                    endDate: new Date('11/21/2013'),
                    description: '''This conference will bring coders from
                                across platforms, languages, and industries
                                together for an exciting day of tips, tricks,
                                and tech!  Stay sharp!  Stay at the top of your
                                game!  But, don't stay home!  Come an join us
                                this fall for the first annual Gateway Code
                                Camp.''')
```

```groovy
        if(!event1.save()){
            event1.errors.allErrors.each{error ->
                println "An error occured with event1: ${error}"
            }
        }
        def event2 = new TekEvent(name: 'Perl Before Swine',
                        city: 'Austin, MN',
                        organizer: 'John Deere',
                        venue: 'SPAM Museum',
                        startDate: new Date('11/2/2013'),
                        endDate: new Date('11/2/2013'),
                        description: '''Join the Perl programmers of the Pork Producers
                                    of America as we hone our skills and ham it up
                                    a bit.  You can show off your programming chops
                                    while trying to win a year's supply of pork
                                    chops in our programming challenge.

                                    Come and join us in historic (and aromatic),
                                    Austin, Minnesota.  You'll know when you're
                                    there!''')
        if(!event2.save()){
            event2.errors.allErrors.each{error ->
                println "An error occured with event2: ${error}"
            }
        }
    }
    def destroy = {
    }
}
```

Notice the triple single quotes (''') surrounding the description values in our new TekEvent instances. This is a Groovy way to declare a multiline String, which allows us to enter text on multiple lines without joining them with + signs. (It's yet another way that Groovy helps us keep our code cleaner.)

By assigning our new TekEvent instances to a variable and then saving them in a separate step, we're able to do a little error checking in case we mistyped something; when a domain class instance fails to save, its errors property will be populated with one or more Error objects, which will give us some clues as to what went wrong.

Note also the import statement at the beginning of this file. We need this in order to access the classes we've created under the com.tekdays package. It's important to remember to import them, because when we run the create-domain-class script, Grails does *not* insert this statement here for us.

Joe asks:

Why Not Just Use a "Real" Database from the Beginning?

When your Grails application is hooked up to a persistent database, it becomes a little more difficult to make changes to the domain model. Grails will make some updates to your database; for example, it will add new columns based on new properties. But it won't drop columns.

Using the in-memory database for development makes it easier to share your project with other developers, since they don't have to create a database to run your project locally. And if you're working on a team, using the in-memory database with test data loaded in BootStrap.groovy can prevent issues with tests passing on one machine and not another because of data differences.

If you prefer to not use the in-memory database for development, you can jump ahead to *Configuring a Database*, on page 79 for information on hooking up to a MySQL database, in which case you can skip the BootStrap.groovy code altogether.

Once you've saved those changes, run the application again. When we navigate to the list view, it should look more like the following figure.

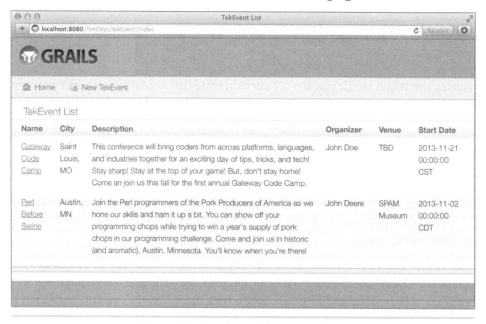

Figure 8—List view with sample data

If your new data doesn't show up, check your console output to see whether anything was reported by our sophisticated error-handling system.

```
if(!event1.save()){
    event1.errors.allErrors.each{error ->
        println "An error occured with event1: ${error}"
    }
}
```

Now that we have some data to look at, we'd like to point out a couple more features of the default list view. The first property in the class—in this case, name, which we put first in our constraints for the TekEvent class—by default becomes a link that will bring up the selected item in the show view. This ensures that when we first run the app with our new data in BootStrap.groovy, we already have an easy way to get around. The other feature is difficult to show on a printed page: all the columns in the table are sortable by clicking the column header. The sort order toggles between ascending and descending as you would expect. Not bad for the amount of code we had to write!

Summary

We're off to a great start. We have the basics of the first three features working: we can create new events, we can edit them, and we can display them (see the next two figures).

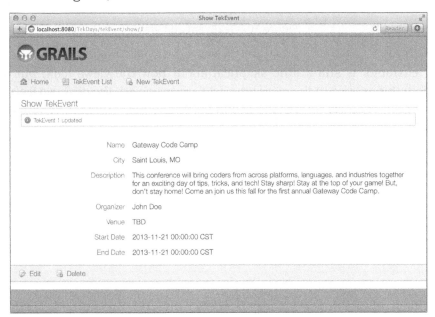

Figure 9—TekEvent show view

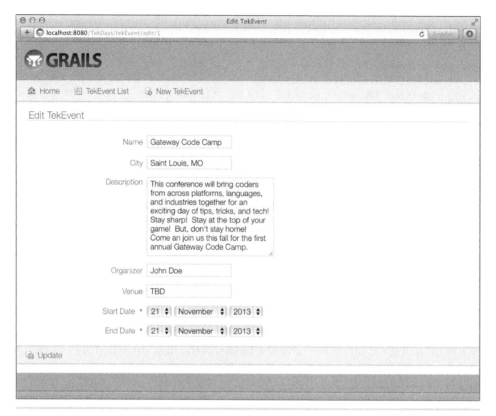

Figure 10—TekEvent edit view

Our customer is still a little skeptical about how the views look, but we'll smooth things over. In the meantime, let's press on with the next two features. In the next chapter, we're going to add users and allow them to volunteer for events.

CHAPTER 4

Building Relationships

In this iteration, we will be adding more domain classes and defining the relationships between them.

The *event* is key to the TekDays application, but we can't have an event without that visionary individual who steps up to organize it and the enthusiastic volunteers who help bring it about. *Organizers* and *volunteers* are two roles that *users* of TekDays will play.

The same user can be an organizer of one event and a volunteer on one or more others. The TekDays domain model will have to reflect these relationships, but it takes more than one to form a relationship. So, we'll start by adding another domain class.

The TekUser Domain Class

Some databases consider User to be a reserved word, so we'll call our class TekUser. (Kind of catchy, huh?) Our TekUser class diagram looks like this:

TekUser
String fullName
String userName
String password
String email
String website
String bio

To create this class, we'll run the create-domain-class script like so:

```
$ grails create-domain-class com.tekdays.TekUser
```

Now open TekDays/grails-app/domain/com/tekdays/TekUser.groovy, and edit it to look like this:

model.0.2/TekDays/grails-app/domain/com/tekdays/TekUser.groovy
```groovy
package com.tekdays

class TekUser {
    String fullName
    String userName
    String password
    String email
    String website
    String bio

    String toString() { fullName }

    static constraints = {
        fullName()
        userName()
        email()
        website()
        bio maxSize:5000
    }
}
```

We added the constraints and toString() method right away this time. Next, we'll create the controller and enable dynamic scaffolding for our TekUser class. Go ahead and run grails create-controller:

```
$ grails create-controller com.tekdays.TekUser
```

Now let's enable the scaffolding:

model.0.2/TekDays/grails-app/controllers/com/tekdays/TekUserController.groovy
```groovy
package com.tekdays

class TekUserController {

    def scaffold = TekUser
}
```

This gives us scaffolded views, like the ones we saw for TekEvent. Before we look at those, let's go ahead and add some test data to make them more interesting. Open TekDays/grails-app/conf/BootStrap.groovy, and add the following code to the init block immediately after the code we added in the previous chapter:

model.0.2/TekDays/grails-app/conf/BootStrap.groovy
```groovy
new TekUser(fullName: 'John Doe',
            userName: 'jdoe',
            password: 't0ps3cr3t',
            email: 'jdoe@johnsgroovyshop.com',
            website: 'blog.johnsgroovyshop.com',
```

```
            bio: '''John has been programming for over 40 years. He has
                    worked with every programming language known to man
                    and has settled on Groovy. In his spare time, John
                    dabbles in astro physics and plays
                    shuffleboard.'''').save()
new TekUser(fullName: 'John Deere',
            userName: 'tractorman',
            password: 't0ps3cr3t',
            email: 'john.deere@porkproducers.org',
            website: 'www.perl.porkproducers.org',
            bio: '''John is a top notch Perl programmer and a pretty
                    good hand around the farm. If he can't program it he
                    can plow it!'''').save()
```

This code is similar to our test data for TekEvent, so we won't spend much time on it. Now when we run TekDays and navigate to the index page, we see a new link for the TekUserController. Follow this link to see the list view, as shown in the next figure.

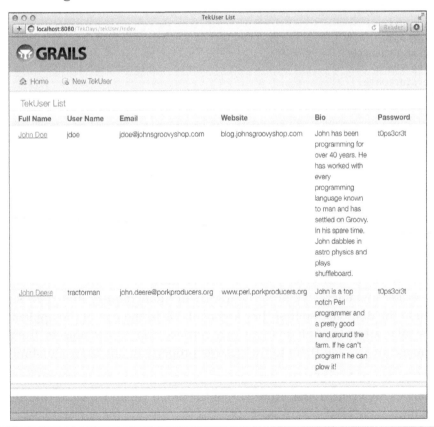

Figure 11—TekUser list view

The generated list views don't show all the properties of our class; by default, the Grails scaffolding produces list views with six columns. Columns are chosen based on the current ordering of properties. (Remember that the property ordering is alphabetical by default but can be changed by adding constraints, as we discussed in *Constraining Our Domain*, on page 30.)

Now that we have two domain classes, we can see how Grails handles domain relationships.

One-to-One Relationships

In Figure 3, *Diagram of the TekEvent class*, on page 22, the organizer property is shown as a TekUser, but in our current TekEvent, it's still a String. Now that we have a TekUser, we can fix this discrepancy. Let's open TekDays/grails-app/domain/com/tekdays/TekEvent.groovy and change the organizer from a String to a TekUser:

```
model.0.2/TekDays/grails-app/domain/com/tekdays/TekEvent.groovy
String city
String name
TekUser organizer
String venue
Date startDate
Date endDate
String description
```

We have now joined the TekEvent and TekUser classes in a *one-to-one* relationship. Each TekEvent instance can have exactly one TekUser. That was simple enough; however, if we save this and try to run our application, we'll get a lovely (and long) error stacktrace.

The problem is that we are still assigning a String ('John Doe' or 'John Deere') to the organizer property of the TekEvent instances that we created in BootStrap.groovy. This will be easy to fix, but we will need to do a bit more coding.

In the init block of BootStrap.groovy, we are creating two TekEvent instances and two TekUser instances. We are creating them anonymously and then saving them to the database so that they are available to the rest of the application. Let's take advantage of this: we can retrieve the TekUser objects from the database and assign them to the organizer property of our TekEvent instances.

For this to work, we'll also have to rearrange our code so that the TekUser instances are created first. Here's an abbreviated version of what this should look like:

```
new TekUser(fullName: 'John Doe',
            userName: 'jdoe',
            password: 't0ps3cr3t',
            email: 'jdoe@johnsgroovyshop.com',
            website: 'blog.johnsgroovyshop.com',
            bio: 'John has been programming for over 40 years. ...').save()

new TekUser(fullName: 'John Deere',
            userName: 'tractorman',
            password: 't0ps3cr3t',
            email: 'john.deere@porkproducers.org',
            website: 'www.perl.porkproducers.org',
            bio: 'John is a top notch Perl programmer and a ...').save()

def event1 = new TekEvent(name: 'Gateway Code Camp',
            city: 'Saint Louis, MO',
            organizer: TekUser.findByFullName('John Doe'),
            venue: 'TBD',
            startDate: new Date('11/21/2013'),
            endDate: new Date('11/21/2013'),
            description: '''This conference will bring
                            coders ...''').save()

def event2 = new TekEvent(name: 'Perl Before Swine',
            city: 'Austin, MN',
            organizer: TekUser.findByFullName('John Deere'),
            venue: 'SPAM Museum',
            startDate: new Date('11/2/2013'),
            endDate: new Date('11/2/2013'),
            description: 'Join the Perl programmers of the ...').save()
```

Introducing GORM

What we just did is almost trivial as far as code goes but very interesting behind the scenes. To set the value for the organizer property of each TekEvent, we are calling the method TekUser.findByFullName(). This method doesn't actually exist. We mentioned earlier that Grails adds methods to our domain classes at runtime. This is not one of them. Instead, what Grails is doing here is *synthesizing behavior at runtime*. When a method call beginning with *findBy* is made on one of our domain classes, Grails will parse the rest of the method name to see whether it matches any of the properties of the class. Then it executes the behavior that we would expect if a method with that name and parameters *did* exist. This is called a *dynamic finder*, and it is part of one of Grails' core components called Grails Object Relational Mapping (GORM).

Any time we save, retrieve, or relate any of our domain class instances, we are using GORM. GORM removes the need for much of the boilerplate, repetitive code that we would have to write to work with other ORM systems or JDBC.[1] We'll learn more about GORM and take advantage of more of its features as we continue working on TekDays.

The code we added hooks up TekEvent and TekUser in a unidirectional one-to-one relationship. A TekEvent *has a* TekUser, but the TekUser doesn't know anything about the TekEvent.

Now that we have a domain relationship, let's take a look at it. Run the application, and follow the TekEventController link. Then click the name of one of the events to bring up the show view. It should look similar to what is shown in the next figure. Notice that the organizer's full name now appears as a link. This link takes us to the TekUser show view.

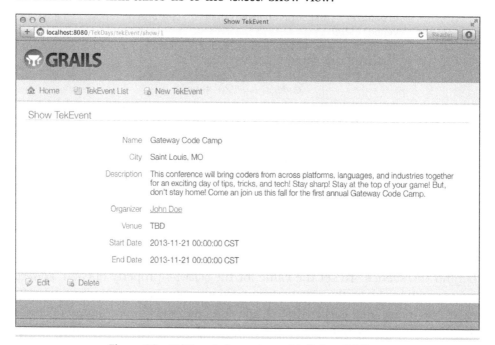

Figure 12—**TekEvent** show view with link to **TekUser**

Keeping Our Tests Updated

If we've been running our tests frequently with grails test-app (and we should be), we will see that our TekEventSpec fails.

---

1. Java Database Connectivity.

Dynamic Finders

As we mentioned in *Metaprogramming*, on page 9, Grails takes advantage of Groovy's metaprogramming capabilities to *synthesize* finders for our domain class properties at runtime. We can call methods that begin with *findBy*, *findAllBy*, or *countBy*, followed by one or more properties and optional operators.

Some examples will make this clearer. All of these would be valid methods on TekEvent:

- countByCity('New York')
- findAllByStartDateGreaterThan(new Date())
- findByCityAndDescriptionLike("Minneapolis", "%Groovy%")

Properties in dynamic finders can be joined by And or Or. The following are some of the operators that can be used:

- LessThan
- Between
- IsNotNull
- Like

For a complete list of operators, see http://www.grails.org/OperatorNamesInDynamicMethods.

That's because the test code still expects TekEvent.organizer to be a String. Let's fix that before we move on.

We don't really want to include the TekUser class in the unit test for TekEvent, so instead, we'll mock the organizer with a Map. Open TekDays/test/unit/com/tekdays/TekEventSpec.groovy, and change the organizer property, as shown here:

model.1.2/TekDays/test/unit/com/tekdays/TekEventSpec.groovy
```groovy
package com.tekdays

import grails.test.mixin.TestFor
import spock.lang.Specification

/**
 * See the API for {@link grails.test.mixin.domain.DomainClassUnitTestMixin}
 * for usage instructions
 */

@TestFor(TekEvent)
class TekEventSpec extends Specification {

    def setup() {
    }

    def cleanup() {
    }
```

```
void "test toString"() {
      when: "a tekEvent has a name and a city"
            def tekEvent = new TekEvent(name:'Groovy One',
                                 city: 'San Francisco',
➤                                organizer: [fullName: 'John Doe']
➤                                   as TekUser)

      then: "the toString method will combine them."
            tekEvent.toString() == 'Groovy One, San Francisco'
}

}
```

Groovy allows us to coerce a Map to a class or interface with the as operator. We're giving the Map a fullName element for clarity, but we could just as well have used an empty Map, since we're not referring to any of the organizer's properties in our test.

Now our tests pass and all is well.

One-to-Many Relationships

A TekEvent will have one organizer but will need more than one volunteer to be successful. A volunteer is also a TekUser, and we just set up a relationship between TekEvent and TekUser. We're going to set up another relationship between these two classes, but this time it will be a one-to-many relationship. A TekEvent will have zero or more volunteers.

Grails uses a static property called hasMany to declare one-to-many relationships. hasMany is a Map, with the key being the name of the collection in the owning class and the value being the type of the child class. Let's see how that looks in our TekEvent. Open TekDays/grails-app/domain/com/tekdays/TekEvent.groovy, and add the hasMany declaration, as shown in the following code:

```
model.0.2/TekDays/grails-app/domain/com/tekdays/TekEvent.groovy
Date endDate
String description

➤ static hasMany = [volunteers : TekUser]

String toString(){
  "$name, $city"
}
```

That line of code—static hasMany = [volunteers : TekUser]—gives us a Collection of TekUser objects, along with methods to add and remove them. Grails' dynamic scaffolding will automatically pick up this change and modify our views. To demonstrate this, let's add some more bootstrap code. Open TekDays/grails-app/conf/BootStrap.groovy, and add the following code to the bottom of the init block:

`model.0.2/TekDays/grails-app/conf/BootStrap.groovy`

```groovy
def g1 = TekEvent.findByName('Gateway Code Camp')
g1.addToVolunteers(new TekUser(fullName: 'Sarah Martin',
                               userName: 'sarah',
                               password: '54321',
                               email: 'sarah@martinworld.com',
                               website: 'www.martinworld.com',
                               bio: 'Web designer and Grails afficianado.'))
g1.addToVolunteers(new TekUser(fullName: 'Bill Smith',
                               userName: 'Mr_Bill',
                               password: '12345',
                               email: 'mrbill@email.com',
                               website: 'www.mrbillswebsite.com',
                               bio: 'Software developer, claymation artist.'))
g1.save()
```

With this code, we retrieve a TekEvent by calling TekEvent.findByName(). Then we add new TekUser instances with the TekEvent.addToVolunteers() method, which Grails dynamically synthesizes for us. Finally, we save our TekEvent, which also saves its TekUser instances.

When we navigate to the show view for this event, we see that it contains a list of volunteer's names. Each name links to the TekUser show view for that user. (See the following figure.)

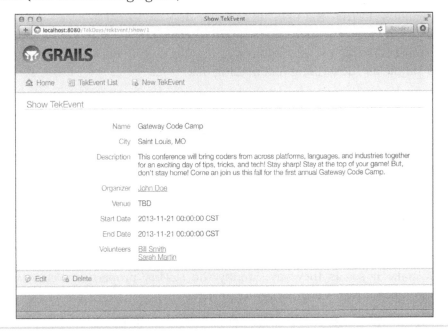

Figure 13—TekEvent show view with volunteers

Grails also supports bidirectional one-to-many relationships with cascading deletes using the static belongsTo[2] property, which is declared in the child class, like so:

```
class Parent {
    ...
    static hasMany = [children : Child]
}
class Child {
    ...
    Parent parent
    static belongsTo = Parent
}
```

Collections of Simple Data Types

We've added an organizer and a collection of volunteers to our TekEvent. That takes care of three more features from our list. We have some time left in this iteration, so let's take on another feature. We'll add the ability for anonymous users to register interest in an event.

On second thought, a completely anonymous show of interest isn't very valuable. Let's say that a person can show an interest by registering to be notified when there are updates to the event. It will still be *somewhat* anonymous, in that the user has to give only an email address. From an application viewpoint, this is also simpler; we won't have to create another domain class to represent this information. For the end user, we'll try to make it as simple as subscribing to a mailing list.

Grails provides a great way for us to associate these addresses with a TekEvent: we can use the hasMany property with a simple data type instead of a domain class. We already used hasMany to set up a collection of TekUser instances named volunteers. This time we will be setting up a String collection containing email addresses.

We need to give a meaningful name to the collection of email addresses—emails is a bit too generic. Sure, these are email addresses, but they represent individuals who have responded to let us know they are interested in an event. We'll go with respondents.

Let's make it so, as they say. Modify the hasMany property in TekDays/grails-app/domain/com/tekdays/TekEvent.groovy to look like this:

```
static hasMany = [volunteers : TekUser, respondents : String]
```

---

2. belongsTo is used to show that another class is the *owning* side of a relationship. It is used for one-to-many and many-to-many relationships.

With this code in place, our TekEvent now has a collection of respondents' email addresses. This change will be reflected in our scaffolded views, but that will be easier to see with some data in place. Open TekDays/grails-app/conf/Boot-Strap.groovy, and add a few calls to TekEvent.addToRespondents(). It should look something like this:

model.1.2/TekDays/grails-app/conf/BootStrap.groovy

```
g1.addToVolunteers(new TekUser(fullName: 'Bill Smith',
                               userName: 'Mr_Bill',
                               password: '12345',
                               email: 'mrbill@email.com',
                               website: 'www.mrbillswebsite.com',
                               bio: 'Software developer, claymation artist.'))

g1.addToRespondents('ben@grailsmail.com')
g1.addToRespondents('zachary@linuxgurus.org')
g1.addToRespondents('solomon@bootstrapwelding.com')

g1.save()
```

This code is similar to the call to TekEvent.addToVolunteers() also shown here.

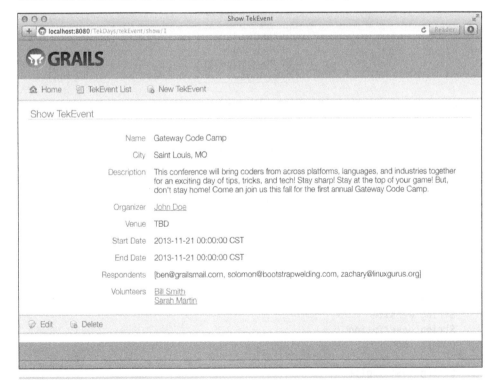

Figure 14—TekEvent show view with respondents

The difference is that we are not creating new domain class instances to pass into the method—we are passing Strings instead. In the next figure, we see how the scaffolding automatically picks up this new relationship and displays it in a reasonable manner. (It's reasonable but not very fashionable. Remember we are focusing on functionality now. We'll spruce it up a bit later.)

Adding a Sponsor Class

TekDays is geared toward community-driven technical conferences, and one of the keys to a successful community-driven conference is low cost to attendees. This can be difficult to accomplish, considering the cost of meeting space, A/V rental, food, and so on. One way to have all these necessities and still keep the registration fees low is to involve *sponsors*; in other words, companies involved in the technology or technologies featured are often willing to contribute toward the cost of the conference in exchange for a bit of exposure.

It sounds like it's time for a new domain class. We'll call our new class Sponsor. (See the following figure.)

Sponsor
String name
String website
String description
byte[] logo

Figure 15—The **Sponsor** class

From our project's root directory, run the following:

```
$ grails create-domain-class com.tekdays.Sponsor
```

Open the newly created TekDays/grails-app/domain/com/tekdays/Sponsor.groovy. Enter the following code:

```
model.2.2/TekDays/grails-app/domain/com/tekdays/Sponsor.groovy
package com.tekdays

class Sponsor {
    String name
    String website
    String description
    byte[] logo

    String toString(){
        name
    }
}
```

```
static constraints = {
    name blank: false
    website blank: false, url: true
    description nullable: true, maxSize: 5000
    logo nullable: true, maxSize: 1000000
}
}
```

There are a few new things to point out in this code. Two of them have to do with the logo property. The first is the logo property's type: byte[]. The logo property will hold an image of the sponsor's logo, which will be stored as an array of bytes. Next is the constraint for logo. We added a maxSize constraint to this property to let the database know to use a blob (or other appropriate data type). Without this, many database systems would produce a field that wouldn't hold anything bigger than an icon. Finally, note the second constraint for the website property: the url constraint ensures that this property will only accept a valid URL.

We also need to create a controller to enable dynamic scaffolding. We'll do this exactly as we did for TekEvent and TekUser, but for a refresher, here it is:

```
$ grails create-controller com.tekdays.Sponsor
```

Next, open the generated controller TekDays/grails-app/controllers/com/tekdays/Sponsor-Controller.groovy, and modify it like so:

model.2.2/TekDays/grails-app/controllers/com/tekdays/SponsorController.groovy
```
package com.tekdays
class SponsorController {
    def scaffold = Sponsor
}
```

When we run TekDays now, we see a new SponsorController link. Follow that link to the empty list view, and then click "New Sponsor" to open the create view. In Figure 16, *Sponsor create view*, on page 50, we see that the logo property is rendered as a *file input* element. But Grails goes beyond that: full file upload functionality is baked right in. When we save a new Sponsor, the file we've chosen for the logo will automatically be uploaded and stored in the database. After we save, we can see that the show view doesn't look that great, but we'll work on that later.

Many-to-Many Relationships

One of the concerns about bringing in a sponsor for a technical event is that the whole thing might turn into a commercial for a vendor. That becomes much less of a concern if there are multiple sponsors for an event. On the other hand, a single company might be interested in sponsoring more than

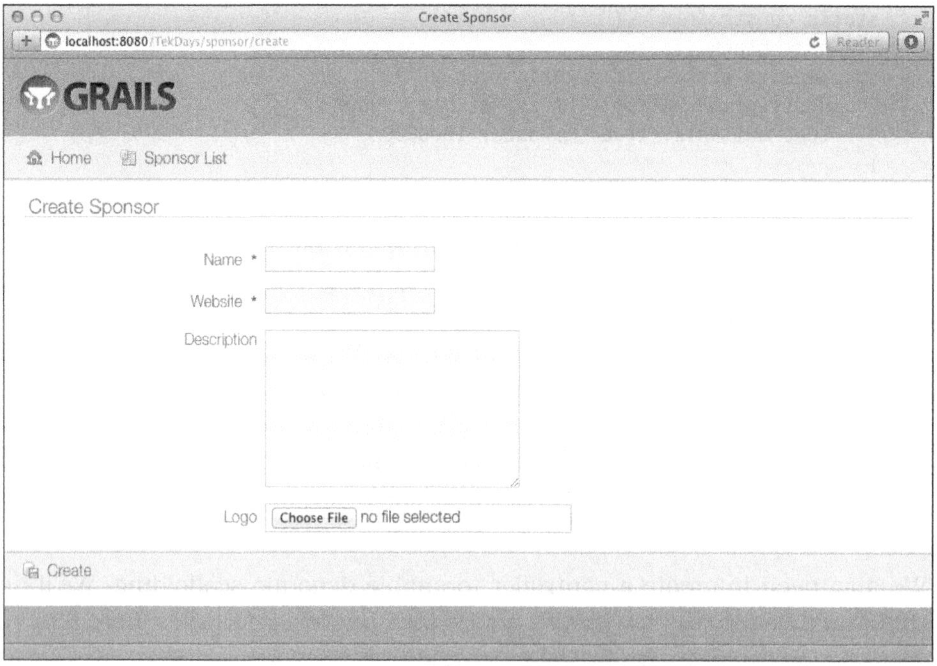

Figure 16—Sponsor create view

one event. So, should a TekEvent have a collection of Sponsor instances, or should Sponsor have a collection of TekEvent instances? The short answer is *both*. The longer answer, which we'll get to shortly, is *neither*.

The relationship between TekEvent and Sponsor is a *many-to-many* relationship. Grails supports many-to-many relationships implicitly by having each class include the other in its hasMany block. In this arrangement, each class will have a collection of the other, but one side has to be declared as the owning side. For this, Grails uses the static variable belongsTo.

Here's an example:

```
class TekEvent {
    ...
    static hasMany=[..., sponsors : Sponsor]
}

class Sponsor {
    ...
    static hasMany=[events : TekEvent]
    static belongsTo = TekEvent
}
```

This code would create the relationships, or links, between a TekEvent and its collection of Sponsor instances, as well as between a Sponsor and its collection of TekEvent instances. What it wouldn't do is tell us anything about the *relationship* itself. When our users are organizing an event, it's great that they're able to see who their sponsors are, but it would also be helpful to know *what* each sponsor is contributing. Are they providing the meeting space, A/V equipment, food, T-shirts (a critical piece of a successful event), or a cash contribution? If they are contributing cash, how much?

To store this type of information, we will need an intermediary class. We'll call this class Sponsorship. (See the following figure.)

Figure 17—The Sponsorship class

This class will have a reference to a single TekEvent and a single Sponsor, with fields to tell us more about what the sponsor is providing for the event. Let's go ahead and create this class:

```
$ grails create-domain-class com.tekdays.Sponsorship
```

We'll implement this class with the following code:

model.3.2/TekDays/grails-app/domain/com/tekdays/Sponsorship.groovy
```groovy
package com.tekdays

class Sponsorship {
    TekEvent event
    Sponsor sponsor
    String contributionType
    String description
    String notes

    static constraints = {
        event nullable: false
        sponsor nullable: false
        contributionType inList:["Other", "Venue", "A/V", "Promotion", "Cash"]
        description nullable: true, blank: true
        notes nullable: true, blank: true, maxSize: 5000
    }
}
```

In this class, we're using a new constraint. The inList constraint takes as its value a list of Strings. Only values matching one of the items in the list will be allowed; any other values will cause a constraint violation when saving. But wait, there's more. Grails will also use this constraint to render an HTML <select> element in the scaffolded views. We'll take a look at that shortly, but first we have a little more plumbing to do.

We need to modify TekEvent and Sponsor so they each have a collection of Sponsorship instances. Open TekDays/grails-app/domain/com/tekdays/Sponsor.groovy, and add a hasMany property. Then add a new constraint to the constraints block, like so:

model.3.2/TekDays/grails-app/domain/com/tekdays/Sponsor.groovy

```
static hasMany = [sponsorships : Sponsorship]

static constraints = {
    name blank: false
    website blank: false, url: true
    description nullable: true, maxSize: 5000
    logo nullable: true, maxSize: 1000000
    sponsorships nullable: true
}
```

Repeat those steps with TekDays/grails-app/domain/com/tekdays/TekEvent.groovy:

model.2.2/TekDays/grails-app/domain/com/tekdays/TekEvent.groovy

```
static hasMany = [volunteers : TekUser,
                  respondents : String,
                  sponsorships : Sponsorship]

static constraints = {
    name()
    city()
    description maxSize: 5000
    organizer()
    venue()
    startDate()
    endDate()
    volunteers nullable: true
    sponsorships nullable: true
}
```

One last step: let's add some sponsorship data in our BootStrap so that we'll have something to look at. Open TekDays/grails-app/conf/BootStrap.groovy, and add the following code to the bottom of the init block:

model.2.2/TekDays/grails-app/conf/BootStrap.groovy

```
def s1 = new Sponsor(name:'Contegix',
                     website:'http://www.contegix.com',
                     description:'Beyond Managed Hosting for your
                               Enterprise').save()
```

```
def s2 = new Sponsor(name:'Object Computing Incorporated',
                     website:'http://ociweb.com',
                     description:'An OO Software Engineering Company'
                     ).save()
def sp1 = new Sponsorship(event:g1,
                          sponsor:s1,
                          contributionType:'Other',
                          description:'Cool T-Shirts').save()
def sp2 = new Sponsorship(event:g1,
                          sponsor:s2,
                          contributionType:'Venue',
                          description:'Will be paying for the
                                      Moscone').save()
```

When we run the application and navigate to the TekEvent show view, we see
something like the following figure.

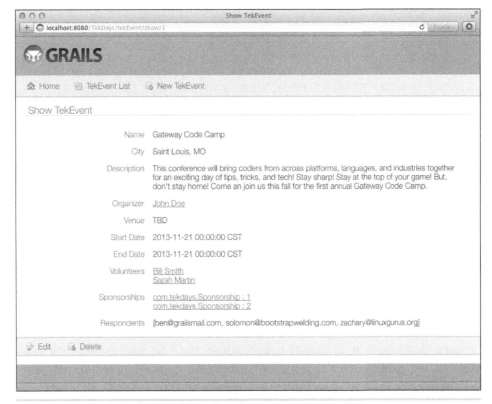

Figure 18—TekEvent show view with sponsorships

Notice that the Sponsorship instances are shown as com.tekdays.Sponsorship : 1. This
is because we did not define a toString() for the Sponsorship class. If you're following
along (and we do hope you are), you may also notice that clicking the

Constraints and Validation

Constraints are used in generating scaffolded views for a domain class as well as for hints in generating the database schema. But the real power of constraints is the part they play in validation. When we call save() or validate() on one of our domain class instances, Grails will try to validate the instance against any constraints we have assigned. If any of the constraints are not met, the save() or validate() call will fail, and appropriate error information will be stored in the instance's errors[a] property.

Grails provides several handy constraints that we can take advantage of, but it also gives us the ability to define custom constraints,[b] so the possibilities are endless. Here are some of the more useful built-in constraints:

- blank (true/false): Allows an empty string value.
- nullable (true/false): Allows null values.
- max: Specifies the maximum value.
- min: Specifies the minimum value.
- vsize: Takes a Groovy range to determine bounds.
- maxSize: Specifies the maximum size of a String or Collection.
- minSize: Specifies the minimum size of a String or Collection.
- inList: Only allows values contained in the supplied list.
- matches: Requires value to match a regular expression.
- unique (true/false): Enforces uniqueness in the database.
- url (true/false): Only accepts a valid URL.
- email (true/false): Only accepts a valid email address.
- creditCard (true/false): Only accepts a valid credit card number.
- validator: Takes a closure for custom validation. The first parameter is the value, and the second (optional) parameter is the instance being validated.

---

a.   Error details can be found via allErrors:

```
errors.allErrors.each{
    //iterate over errors
}
```

b.   See http://grails.org/doc/2.3.1/ref/Constraints/validator.html.

Sponsorship link leads to an error page. This is because we haven't created a SponsorshipController to enable the scaffolding. We'll be addressing this soon. Also, as we go about cleaning up our user interface, we'll have different ways to display a Sponsorship, depending on the context; but for now, this serves to show us that the one-to-many relationship is established correctly. Well done!

Finishing Up the Domain Model

Looking again at our feature list, we can see that we'll need two more domain classes. We're going to have a list of *tasks* that need to be done to prepare for an event. That will require a Task class. We're also going to have a simple forum that the organizer and volunteers can use to communicate throughout the process. For this, we will need another class, which we will call TekMessage (Grails already uses message; for example, in its generated views). For a view of these classes, see the following figure.

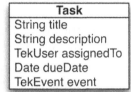

Task
String title
String description
TekUser assignedTo
Date dueDate
TekEvent event

TekMessage
String subject
String content
Message parent
TekEvent event
TekUser author

Figure 19—The Task and TekMessage classes

We'll create the Task class first. Run grails create-domain-class com.tekdays.Task, and add the following code to TekDays/grails-app/domain/com/tekdays/Task.groovy:

model.2.2/TekDays/grails-app/domain/com/tekdays/Task.groovy
```
package com.tekdays
class Task {
    String title
    String notes
    TekUser assignedTo
    Date dueDate
    TekEvent event
    static constraints = {
        title blank: false
        notes blank: true, nullable: true, maxSize: 5000
        assignedTo nullable: true
        dueDate nullable: true
    }
    static belongsTo = TekEvent
}
```

Next we'll create the TekMessage class and add the following code to TekDays/grails-app/domain/com/tekdays/TekMessage.groovy:

model.2.2/TekDays/grails-app/domain/com/tekdays/TekMessage.groovy
```
package com.tekdays

class TekMessage {
    String subject
    String content
    TekMessage parent
    TekEvent event
    TekUser author
```

```
    static constraints = {
        subject blank: false
        content blank: false, maxSize: 2000
        parent nullable: true
        author nullable: false
    }
    static belongsTo = TekEvent
}
```

There's not much to look at in these classes other than the belongsTo. You'll notice that both of these classes have the following line: static belongsTo = TekEvent. This is because these classes will be involved in bidirectional one-to-many relationships with the TekEvent class, and we want cascading deletes. For example, we know that a TekMessage will belong to only one TekEvent, and if that TekEvent goes away, there is no reason to keep the TekMessage.

To complete these relationships, we will need to once again modify our TekEvent class. We'll modify the hasMany property and add two more constraints to TekDays/grails-app/domain/com/tekdays/TekEvent.groovy.

Since we've made so many changes to this class, we'll show the whole thing here for the sake of clarity. Note the highlighted lines:

model.3.2/TekDays/grails-app/domain/com/tekdays/TekEvent.groovy
```
package com.tekdays

class TekEvent {
    String city
    String name
    TekUser organizer
    String venue
    Date startDate
    Date endDate
    String description

    String toString(){
      "$name, $city"
    }

    static hasMany = [volunteers : TekUser,
                      respondents : String,
                      sponsorships : Sponsorship,
➤                     tasks : Task,
➤                     messages : TekMessage]

    static constraints = {
        name()
        city()
        description maxSize: 5000
```

```
        organizer()
        venue()
        startDate()
        endDate()
        volunteers nullable: true
        sponsorships nullable: true
➤       tasks nullable: true
➤       messages nullable: true
    }

}
```

Summary

In this iteration, we created our domain model, defined and discussed the relationships between various classes in our model, and set up bootstrap data that we can use to bring our model to life during development.

Now that we have our domain model set up the way we want, we are ready to generate the code that will enable us to make more significant changes in our application. In the next chapter, we'll generate and review the code behind all of the functionality we've seen so far.

CHAPTER 5

Beyond Scaffolding

So far, our TekDays application contains six persistent domain classes, three controllers, and twelve views—and all with less than 190 lines of code. Now, Grails uses the Groovy programming language, and Groovy is known for its conciseness, but even in Groovy, this much functionality takes more than 190 lines of code. In fact, it's Grails' dynamic scaffolding that is creating all this for us at runtime. Scaffolding is a great feature; we've been taking advantage of it to gradually build and tweak our domain model, and all the while we've been able to see the effects in our views. However, it's time to remove the training wheels and start taking control of our code.

Generating Scaffolding Code

Grails gives us an easy way to generate the code that does what the dynamic scaffolding has been doing for us. We won't see any changes to the application, but we will have the code necessary to make changes. To get started, we will use the grails generate-all script.

The generate-all script can be called in a few different ways. If you call it with no arguments, you will be prompted for a name. (By convention, this would be a domain class name.) For the more argumentative types, you can call generate-all with a name as the argument. Both of these approaches generate a controller, four .gsp view files, and a *template*, which is also a .gsp file. (We'll have a detailed discussion on templates in *Of Templates and Ajax*, on page 108.) This second method is what we usually use after creating a new domain class, but since right now we have several domain classes for which we want to generate corresponding controllers and views, we will use a third option. Sometimes referred to as *uber-generate-all*, this modification to the generate-all script was contributed by Marcel Overdijk.[1] Let's try it:

---

1. http://marceloverdijk.blogspot.com/

```
$ grails generate-all "*"
```

Once this script gets going, it will prompt you to confirm the replacement of the controllers and controller tests that we created earlier. Go ahead and let them be replaced. We won't need the old ones anymore. When it's done, you'll see the statement Finished generation for domain classes.

If we run the application now, we will have all the features that we had before we generated the code and then some. You may recall that we created controllers and enabled dynamic scaffolding for only three of our domain classes (TekEvent, TekUser, and Sponsor). We now have controllers for Sponsorship, Task, and TekMessage. We may not end up keeping all of this generated code, but it makes a great learning tool, and these files can serve as stubs to which we can add custom code. Let's take a closer look at the code we've generated.

Anatomy of a Grails Controller

Let's examine the TekEventController first: what is it doing for us, and what else we can do with it? Open TekDays/grails-app/controllers/com/tekdays/TekEventController.groovy, and follow along as we take a look at it in chunks:

beyond.2/TekDays/grails-app/controllers/com/tekdays/TekEventController.groovy
```groovy
package com.tekdays

import static org.springframework.http.HttpStatus.*
import grails.transaction.Transactional

@Transactional(readOnly = true)
class TekEventController {

    static allowedMethods = [save: "POST", update: "PUT", delete: "DELETE"]

    def index(Integer max) {
        params.max = Math.min(max ?: 10, 100)
        respond TekEvent.list(params),
          model:[tekEventInstanceCount: TekEvent.count()]
    }
```

After the package declaration and a couple of import statements,[2] the first thing we see is the *class declaration.* (The @Transactional annotation causes all of the actions in this controller to be included in a transaction.) A Grails controller is a plain Groovy class. There is nothing to extend, and there are no interfaces to implement. Controllers serve as the entry points into a Grails application.

---

2. The HttpStatus import is for the HTTP status codes returned by some of the generated Grails actions.

The work done by a controller is done in an *action*. Actions are methods or closure properties of the controller. (In the code that Grails generates for us, they are methods.) Controller actions can be accessed via URLs in the pattern: /appname/controllerBaseName/action. The first letter of the controller's name will be lowercased, and the word *Controller* will be left off.

There are four options to properly exit a controller action. We can call the render() method, which is added to all controllers and takes the name of a *view* along with a Map containing any data the view needs. We can call the redirect() method to issue an HTTP redirect to another URL, or the respond() method (used in the generated actions), which looks at the requested content type to determine what to return. (These last two methods are also added to all controllers; we'll look at them more closely in the following sections.) And we can return *null*, or a Map containing data, which is referred to as a *model*. In this last case, Grails will attempt to render a view with the same name as the action. It will look for this view in a directory named after the root name of the controller; for example, returning from the index action of the TekEventController will cause Grails to render the view /grails-app/views/tekEvent/index.gsp.

The Index Action

The index action is called when we load the TekEvent *list* view. It is the default action that is called when we navigate to this controller. For example, if we follow the link on the default home page for the TekEventController, we'll be calling http://localhost:8080/TekDays/tekEvent. This will call the index action.

The first line of the index action is working with the params property, which is a Map that contains all the parameters of the incoming request. Since it is a Groovy Map, any element to which we assign a value will be added if it doesn't exist.

Take a look at the following line:

```
params.max = Math.min(max ?: 10, 100)
```

In this code, we see the max element being added to the params. The value that is being set is the return value of the Math.min() method. Math.min() is being passed the index method's max argument, if it was given one, or the default of 10, along with the constant of 100. This is just a bit of protection that Grails gives us against trying to pull too many items at once. If we tried to access this view with http://localhost:8080/TekDays/tekEvent/index?max=1000, we would get only 100 results (assuming we had that many events entered—and why not think big?).

The last line calls respond(), which will use Grails' built-in support for content negotiation[3] to determine the format in which to send back our data. In this case, the data we're returning is being supplied by a call to TekEvent.list()[4] and is being returned to our view as HTML. The list() is being passed the params Map, from which it will pull any parameters that it can use.[5] Notice the model argument being given to respond(): this method can, in the case of an HTML response being rendered, take the two arguments model and view, and the index action is passing a model with the key tekEventInstanceCount, which contains the result of TekEvent.count(). This value will be used in the pagination built into the list view, which we will look at shortly.

The end result of the list action is that the list view is rendered using the data returned by respond(). This is done using the conventions we discussed earlier. It's important to note that this feature is not limited to the generated actions and views: as we'll see in Chapter 9, *Big-Picture Views*, on page 131, we can create custom actions and views, and if we follow the conventions, it will just work!

The Show Action

beyond.2/TekDays/grails-app/controllers/com/tekdays/TekEventController.groovy
```groovy
def show(TekEvent tekEventInstance) {
    respond tekEventInstance
}
```

The show action takes a TekEvent instance as a parameter. When an action takes a domain class instance as a parameter, Grails looks for an id in the request, and then looks up the instance with that id. In the show action, respond() returns this instance, and the action then renders the show view.

The Create Action

create is another single-line action:

beyond.2/TekDays/grails-app/controllers/com/tekdays/TekEventController.groovy
```groovy
def create() {
    respond new TekEvent(params)
}
```

---

3. See http://en.wikipedia.org/wiki/Content_negotiation.
4. list() is one of the dynamic methods added to our domain classes. See *More About Domain Classes*, on page 23.
5. This brings up another powerful feature of Grails. Many methods in Grails take a Map as a parameter. These methods will look in the Map for the elements they need and ignore the rest. That means that in one action we can pass the params Map to several different methods, and each will just take from it what it needs. Pretty cool, huh?

Here, respond() returns a newly-created TekEvent instance, assigning any values in the params property to the corresponding properties of the instance. (We'll see why this is done shortly.) The action ends by rendering the create view.

The Save Action

beyond.2/TekDays/grails-app/controllers/com/tekdays/TekEventController.groovy
```
@Transactional
def save(TekEvent tekEventInstance) {
    if (tekEventInstance == null) {
        notFound()
        return
    }

    if (tekEventInstance.hasErrors()) {
        respond tekEventInstance.errors, view:'create'
        return
    }

    tekEventInstance.save flush:true

    request.withFormat {
        form {
            flash.message = message(code: 'default.created.message',
              args: [message(code: 'tekEventInstance.label',
              default: 'TekEvent'), tekEventInstance.id])
            redirect tekEventInstance
        }
        '*' { respond tekEventInstance, [status: CREATED] }
    }
}
```

Like the show action, the save action takes a TekEvent instance as a parameter. (The use of @Transactional on this action omits the readOnly element which we saw set to true at the beginning of the class; by default, it is false.) The save action is called from the create view and begins by checking to see whether there was an instance with the provided id. If there isn't, it calls notFound() (a method generated as part of the controller—we'll discuss it shortly) and exits. If there *is* an instance, the action checks for validation errors by calling hasErrors() on the instance, re-rendering the view to display them if any are found. (Note the view parameter being passed to respond() in the case of validation errors.) If we have an error-free TekEvent instance, we save it to the database.[6]

---

6. Adding flush:true to any persistence-related call will force Hibernate to pass the change on to the data source. It's not usually necessary but good to know about when you need it.

We then call the withFormat()[7] method on the request. form is used in the case of a form submission; in this case, when the form in the create view is submitted and we save the resulting TekEvent instance, we use the <g:message> tag,[8] called as a method, to store a "success" message in the flash Map.[9] We then call redirect(), passing it our new tekEventInstance. This will send us to the show action. (For all other content types, we respond() with the new tekEventInstance and an HTTP status 201—CREATED.)

The Edit Action

beyond.2/TekDays/grails-app/controllers/com/tekdays/TekEventController.groovy
```
def edit(TekEvent tekEventInstance) {
    respond tekEventInstance
}
```

The edit action doesn't do any editing itself: that's left up to the update action. Instead, edit loads up the necessary data and passes it to the edit view. Except for the name (which determines the view rendered), the edit action is identical to the show action.

The Update Action

The update action steps up to bat when changes from the edit view are submitted.

beyond.2/TekDays/grails-app/controllers/com/tekdays/TekEventController.groovy
```
@Transactional

def update(TekEvent tekEventInstance) {
    if (tekEventInstance == null) {
        notFound()
        return
    }

    if (tekEventInstance.hasErrors()) {
        respond tekEventInstance.errors, view:'edit'
        return
    }

    tekEventInstance.save flush:true
```

---

7. See http://grails.org/doc/2.3.1/ref/Controllers/withFormat.html.
8. See http://grails.org/doc/2.3.1/ref/Tags/message.html.
9. flash is often referred to as a *scope*. It's more accurate to refer to it as a Map that exists in a special scope. Values stored in flash are available for this request and one following request, which allows us to store a message before redirecting and have that message be available to the redirected view.

```
    request.withFormat {
        form {
            flash.message = message(code: 'default.updated.message',
              args: [message(code: 'TekEvent.label', default: 'TekEvent'),
              tekEventInstance.id])
            redirect tekEventInstance
        }
        '*'{ respond tekEventInstance, [status: OK] }
    }
}
```

Like earlier actions, update tries to retrieve the TekEvent instance passed to it as an argument. If the instance hasErrors(), we use respond() to direct back to the edit view and display them. The update action finishes in the same way as does the save action, differing only in the "success" message that is stored in flash (an "updated" message rather than a "created" message) and in the HTTP status returned after a successful save() (200 OK).

The Delete Action

The delete action is available, by default, in the edit and show views. It must be called via a DELETE method. Going back to the beginning of our TekEvent-Controller listing, we see the allowedMethods property. This is a Map containing actions and the HTTP methods that can be used to call them. This prevents a user from entering something like http://localhost:8080/TekDays/tekEvent/delete/1 and deleting our event.

beyond.2/TekDays/grails-app/controllers/com/tekdays/TekEventController.groovy
```
@Transactional
def delete(TekEvent tekEventInstance) {

    if (tekEventInstance == null) {
        notFound()
        return
    }

    tekEventInstance.delete flush:true

    request.withFormat {
        form {
            flash.message = message(code: 'default.deleted.message',
              args: [message(code: 'TekEvent.label', default: 'TekEvent'),
              tekEventInstance.id])
            redirect action:"index", method:"GET"
        }
        '*'{ render status: NO_CONTENT }
    }
}
```

The delete action starts out much like the save and update actions—attempting to retrieve a TekEvent instance and calling notFound() if it can't find one. If an instance *is* found, we delete it and then redirect to the index action with a "success" message (or return the status NO_CONTENT). There is no delete view, for obvious reasons.

The notFound() Method

beyond.2/TekDays/grails-app/controllers/com/tekdays/TekEventController.groovy
```
protected void notFound() {
    request.withFormat {
        form {
            flash.message = message(code: 'default.not.found.message',
              args: [message(code: 'tekEventInstance.label',
              default: 'TekEvent'), params.id])
            redirect action: "index", method: "GET"
        }
        '*'{ render status: NOT_FOUND }
    }
}
```

As we can see here, the notFound() method simply makes the same use of with-Format() that we've been seeing in the generated actions. (Having this split out into its own separate method like this means that any of our actions can return NOT_FOUND without having to duplicate this code.) Its form stores a "not found" message in the flash Map and redirects to the index action. For other content types, it simply returns NOT_FOUND.

So, that's a tour of a generated Grails controller. We looked at only one of the six controllers generated by the generate-all script, but they all just have the same code with different domain classes. Feel free to browse the rest of them. It should all look very familiar. Now we'll see what Grails gives us for views.

Grails Views with Groovy Server Pages

Grails uses Groovy Server Pages (GSP) for its view layer. If you've ever worked with JavaServer Pages, well, you have my sympathy, but GSP will seem familiar—only easier to work with. Grails also uses SiteMesh,[10] the page decoration framework from OpenSymphony, to assist in the page layout. SiteMesh will merge each of our .gsp files into a file called main.gsp (located in TekDays/grails-app/views/layouts. This is what gives a consistent look to all of our pages, as we saw with the dynamic scaffolding. We'll begin our tour of the generated views with main.gsp, followed by the four views and the template

---

10. http://wiki.sitemesh.org/display/sitemesh/Home

generated for the TekEvent class. Then we'll look at a couple of the other views that take advantage of additional Grails features.

Exploring main.gsp

```
<!DOCTYPE html>
<!--[if lt IE 7 ]> <html lang="en" class="no-js ie6"> <![endif]-->
<!--[if IE 7 ]>    <html lang="en" class="no-js ie7"> <![endif]-->
<!--[if IE 8 ]>    <html lang="en" class="no-js ie8"> <![endif]-->
<!--[if IE 9 ]>    <html lang="en" class="no-js ie9"> <![endif]-->
<!--[if (gt IE 9)|!(IE)]><!-->
  <html lang="en" class="no-js"><!--<![endif]-->
  <head>
    <meta http-equiv="Content-Type" content="text/html; charset=UTF-8">
    <meta http-equiv="X-UA-Compatible" content="IE=edge,chrome=1">
    <title><g:layoutTitle default="Grails"/></title>
    <meta name="viewport" content="width=device-width, initial-scale=1.0">
    <link rel="shortcut icon" href="${resource(dir: 'images', file:
      'favicon.ico')}" type="image/x-icon">
    <link rel="apple-touch-icon" href="${resource(dir: 'images', file:
      'apple-touch-icon.png')}">
    <link rel="apple-touch-icon" sizes="114x114"
      href="${resource(dir: 'images',
      file: 'apple-touch-icon-retina.png')}">
    <link rel="stylesheet" href="${resource(dir: 'css', file: 'main.css')}"
      type="text/css">
    <link rel="stylesheet" href="${resource(dir: 'css', file: 'mobile.css')}"
      type="text/css">
    <g:layoutHead/>
    <r:layoutResources />
  </head>
  <body>
    <div id="grailsLogo" role="banner"><a href="http://grails.org"><img
      src="${resource(dir: 'images', file: 'grails_logo.png')}" alt="Grails"/>
      </a></div>
    <g:layoutBody/>
    <div class="footer" role="contentinfo"></div>
    <div id="spinner" class="spinner" style="display:none;">
      <g:message code="spinner.alt" default="Loading&hellip;"/></div>
    <g:javascript library="application"/>
    <r:layoutResources />
  </body>
</html>
```

main.gsp starts out with some conditional comments for various versions of Microsoft's Internet Explorer (one for each user)[11] and a couple of HTML <meta> tags. Next is a <title> in the <head> section. This tag contains a <g:layoutTitle>

---

11. See http://msdn.microsoft.com/en-us/library/ms537512(VS.85).aspx.

tag, which will substitute the <title> from the view that is being merged. After another <meta> tag it links in a style sheet and favicon[12] that will be used by all views (it also includes a couple of special icons for Apple devices running iOS). Then there is the <g:layoutHead> tag. This will merge in the contents of the target view's <head> section. The <body> section contains an application logo,[13] a <g:layoutBody> tag, which merges in the <body> contents of the target view, and a <div> with the CSS class footer. This last <div> contains a spinner image and also—along with the <head> section—contains an <r:layoutResources> tag, which tells Grails' Resources framework[14] to include any resources that the target view has required using the <r:require> tag. (We'll see an example of this tag later on.)

As you can see, this file gives us a convenient place to make some major improvements to our application. And that's just what we're going to do, as soon as we finish our tour. As we discuss the four generated views and the template, we will be looking at only portions of them, for the sake of space. We'll give you the name and path for each file so you can open each one on your system and follow along.

The List View

The TekEvent list view is shown in Figure 20, *TekEvent list view*, on page 69. You can refer to that image as we look at the GSP code behind it. You'll find this code in TekDays/grails-app/views/tekEvent/index.gsp.

```
<li><a class="home" href="${createLink(uri: '/')}"><g:message
  code="default.home.label"/></a></li>
<li><g:link class="create" action="create"><g:message
  code="default.new.label" args="[entityName]" /></g:link></li>
```

This code creates the button bar just below the Grails logo. We can see two ways that Grails provides for creating links. The createLink() method takes a relative path and creates a URL, which is assigned to the href attribute of an anchor tag. The <g:link> tag creates an anchor tag using the values of the controller, action, and id attributes (if they're provided). If a controller is not provided, the current controller is assumed. In this case, a link to the create action of the TekEventController will be created. The text for the links is provided by the <g:message> tag, which we saw being used in *The Save Action*, on page 63.

---

12. http://en.wikipedia.org/wiki/Favicon
13. role is an HTML attribute that is used by screen readers to identify the function of a particular element. See http://www.w3.org/TR/xhtml-role/.
14. See http://grails.org/doc/2.3.1/guide/theWebLayer.html#resources.

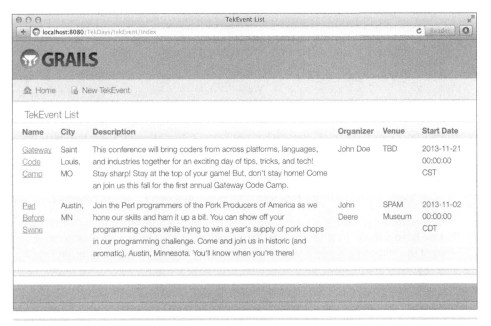

Figure 20—TekEvent list view

```
<g:if test="${flash.message}">
  <div class="message" role="status">${flash.message}</div>
</g:if>
```

This code doesn't show up in our figure above, but it is important to take note of. Recall that during our discussion of controllers, we often had code that would store text in the message element of flash. This is where that text will show up. The <g:if> tag checks for the existence of flash.message and, if found, displays it.

```
<g:sortableColumn property="name" title="${message(code:
  'tekEvent.name.label', default: 'Name')}" />
<g:sortableColumn property="city" title="${message(code:
  'tekEvent.city.label', default: 'City')}" />
<g:sortableColumn property="description" title="${message(code:
  'tekEvent.description.label', default: 'Description')}" />

<th><g:message code="tekEvent.organizer.label" default="Organizer" />
</th>

<g:sortableColumn property="venue" title="${message(code:
  'tekEvent.venue.label', default: 'Venue')}" />
<g:sortableColumn property="startDate" title="${message(code:
  'tekEvent.startDate.label', default: 'Start Date')}" />
```

> \|/ **Joe asks:**
> ‿͡   # What's Up with the <g:message> Tags Everywhere?
>
> In the generated views, Grails uses the <g:message> GSP tag to read text for labels, buttons, and other elements from *message bundles*, which are contained in grails-app/i18n under our TekDays application directory. Internationalization is built into Grails; message bundles for other languages are also stored in the i18n directory, and contain text for various messages that we will need to show the user in our app. The use of <g:message> here ensures that if somebody were to be using our app with a different locale,[a] our user interface would be presented in the correct language.
>
> Using the message bundles for our application's labels and other text also means that we have a single field to edit if we want to change a particular label or message. Many of the instances of <g:message> in the generated views (columns in the list view's table, for example) provide sensible default text in case of a message not being in our i18n files.
>
> To keep things simple for our example purposes, we won't be making use of internationalized messages for the features we add to the TekDays application. For details on how they can be used in Grails, see the online documentation.[b]
>
> ─────────────
> a.   See http://docs.oracle.com/javase/1.5.0/docs/api/java/util/Locale.html.
> b.   http://grails.org/doc/2.3.1/guide/i18n.html

The <g:sortableColumn> tag is what Grails uses to provide sorting on our list view. Note that, by default, this works only with regular properties, not object references or collections. That is why we see a <th> tag used for the organizer property.

```
<g:each in="${tekEventInstanceList}" status="i" var="tekEventInstance">
  <tr class="${(i % 2) == 0 ? 'even' : 'odd'}">
    <td><g:link action="show" id="${tekEventInstance.id}">
      ${fieldValue(bean: tekEventInstance, field: "name")}</g:link></td>
    <td>${fieldValue(bean: tekEventInstance, field: "city")}</td>
    <td>${fieldValue(bean: tekEventInstance, field: "description")}</td>
    <td>${fieldValue(bean: tekEventInstance, field: "organizer")}</td>
    <td>${fieldValue(bean: tekEventInstance, field: "venue")}</td>
    <td><g:formatDate date="${tekEventInstance.startDate}" /></td>
  </tr>
</g:each>
```

This code is the heart of the list view. We start with the <g:each> tag, which iterates over the list that was passed in from the controller. By convention, this list is named tekEventInstanceList. Each item in the tekEventInstanceList is assigned to the tekEventInstance variable, and the body of the <g:each> tag fills in the table row with the properties of the tekEventInstance. Notice that a Groovy expression is used to determine the CSS class of the <tr>—powerful stuff!

Inside the <td> tags, the fieldValue() method is used to render the value of each TekEvent property. This method retrieves the value from the given field of the given bean—in this case, the tekEventInstance—and also calls the method encodeAsHTML() for us, because that's almost always what we want. (We'll learn about encodeAsHTML() when we look at the show view.)

One property, the last in the list, isn't using the fieldValue() method. startDate is a Date type, so Grails renders it using the <g:formatDate> tag, which handles the conversion from Date to String for us.[15]

```
<div class="pagination">
  <g:paginate total="${tekEventInstanceCount ?: 0}" />
</div>
```

The final portion of the index.gsp we'll look at is another one that we can't see in our figure showing the list view. The <g:paginate> tag would cause pagination buttons to show up at the bottom of the list view if we had enough events displayed to warrant it. This tag uses the count that we passed in from the controller's index action.

The Show View

The show view, pictured in Figure 21, *TekEvent show view*, on page 72, is in TekDays/grails-app/views/tekEvent/show.gsp.

Open this file now as we look at a few interesting sections:

```
<g:if test="${tekEventInstance?.name}">
<li class="fieldcontain">
  <span id="name-label" class="property-label"><g:message
    code="tekEvent.name.label" default="Name" /></span>
    <span class="property-value" aria-labelledby="name-label">
      <g:fieldValue bean="${tekEventInstance}" field="name"/></span>
</li>
</g:if>
<g:if test="${tekEventInstance?.city}">
<li class="fieldcontain">
  <span id="city-label" class="property-label"><g:message
    code="tekEvent.city.label" default="City" /></span>
    <span class="property-value" aria-labelledby="city-label">
      <g:fieldValue bean="${tekEventInstance}" field="city"/></span>
</li>
</g:if>
```

---

15. See http://grails.org/doc/2.3.1/ref/Tags/formatDate.html.

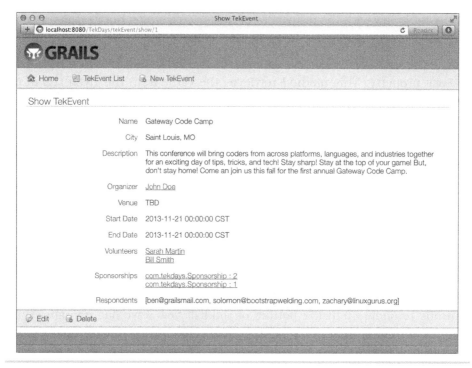

Figure 21—TekEvent show view

The code that displays each property is wrapped in a set of <g:if> tags that check for a value in the property, so that we don't display an empty list item for the property if there's nothing to show. Within this code we see a couple of examples of how Grails displays text properties. Notice the CSS class hierarchy. The <li> tag has a fieldcontain class, and the <span> tags have a property-label or property-value class.[16]

```
<g:if test="${tekEventInstance?.organizer}">
<li class="fieldcontain">
  <span id="organizer-label" class="property-label"><g:message
    code="tekEvent.organizer.label" default="Organizer" /></span>
    <span class="property-value" aria-labelledby="organizer-label">
      <g:link controller="tekUser" action="show"
        id="${tekEventInstance?.organizer?.id}">
          ${tekEventInstance?.organizer?.encodeAsHTML()}</g:link></span>
</li>
</g:if>
```

---

16. aria-labelledby is another HTML attribute used by screen readers—here it refers to the id of the element that is a label for this <span>. See http://www.w3.org/TR/2010/WD-wai-aria-20100916/states_and_properties#aria-labelledby.

Here we have an example of the way Grails displays a related object. The organizer property is rendered as a link to the TekUser show view. The <g:link> tag has its controller and action attributes set accordingly. The id is set to a Groovy expression that reads the id property of the organizer property of the tekEventInstance that we passed in from the controller. Notice the ? after the tekEventInstance and organizer references; this is Groovy's *safe navigation* operator. When this expression is evaluated, if either of these items is null, the whole expression evaluates to null, and no exception is thrown!

Another thing to notice here is the use of the encodeAsHTML() method. This method is added to all String objects and prevents any HTML code from being processed while the page is rendering. This is helpful in defending against cross-site scripting attacks.[17]

```
<g:if test="${tekEventInstance?.volunteers}">
<li class="fieldcontain">
  <span id="volunteers-label" class="property-label"><g:message
    code="tekEvent.volunteers.label" default="Volunteers" /></span>

    <g:each in="${tekEventInstance.volunteers}" var="v">
    <span class="property-value" aria-labelledby="volunteers-label">
      <g:link controller="tekUser" action="show"
        id="${v.id}">${v?.encodeAsHTML()}</g:link></span>
    </g:each>

</li>
</g:if>
```

One-to-many relationships are rendered simply using a <g:each> tag. Here we see the volunteers property being displayed using one property-label <span> and a <span> with class property-value for each item in the collection.

```
<g:if test="${tekEventInstance?.respondents}">
<li class="fieldcontain">
  <span id="respondents-label" class="property-label"><g:message
    code="tekEvent.respondents.label" default="Respondents" /></span>

    <span class="property-value" aria-labelledby="respondents-label">
      <g:fieldValue bean="${tekEventInstance}" field="respondents"/></span>

</li>
</g:if>
```

Rounding out the show view, we have the respondents collection. This property is a collection of String objects containing email addresses. This type of collection is rendered as if it were a single String field. Grails handles converting it

---

17. http://en.wikipedia.org/wiki/Cross-site_scripting

to a comma-separated list, as we see in Figure 21, *TekEvent show view*, on page 72. If we wanted to, we could use a <g:each> tag to show these as a list or in a table.

The Create View

We can see the create view in Figure 22, *TekEvent create view*, on page 75. The code for this view is in TekDays/grails-app/views/tekEvent/create.gsp.

```
<g:hasErrors bean="${tekEventInstance}">
<ul class="errors" role="alert">
  <g:eachError bean="${tekEventInstance}" var="error">
  <li <g:if test="${error in org.springframework.validation.FieldError}">
    data-field-id="${error.field}"</g:if>><g:message error="${error}"/></li>
  </g:eachError>
</ul>
</g:hasErrors>
```

In *The List View*, on page 68, we saw how messages that we set in the controller are displayed in the view. Here we see another type of message block. When a domain instance fails to save, errors are stored in an errors property. The <g:hasErrors> tag is a conditional tag that examines the domain instance assigned to its bean attribute and renders its body if errors are found. In the body of the tag, we find an unordered list populated by a <g:eachError> tag, which works rather like the <g:each> to display the errors in a list at the top of the page. (See Figure 23, *Built-in error handling*, on page 75.)

```
<g:form url="[resource:tekEventInstance, action:'save']" >
```

The <g:form> tag sets up an HTML form. This tag has controller, action, and id (or resource) attributes, which will result in the URL to submit the form to. It can also take a Map—url—that contains these as elements, as we see being done here.

```
<fieldset class="form">
  <g:render template="form"/>
</fieldset>
```

Within the <g:form> tags, we are using the <g:render> tag to (you guessed it) *render* the form template, which is used by both the create and edit views for form elements. (We'll take a look at this template shortly.)

The Edit View

The last of the scaffolded views is the edit view. (See Figure 24, *TekEvent edit view*, on page 76.)

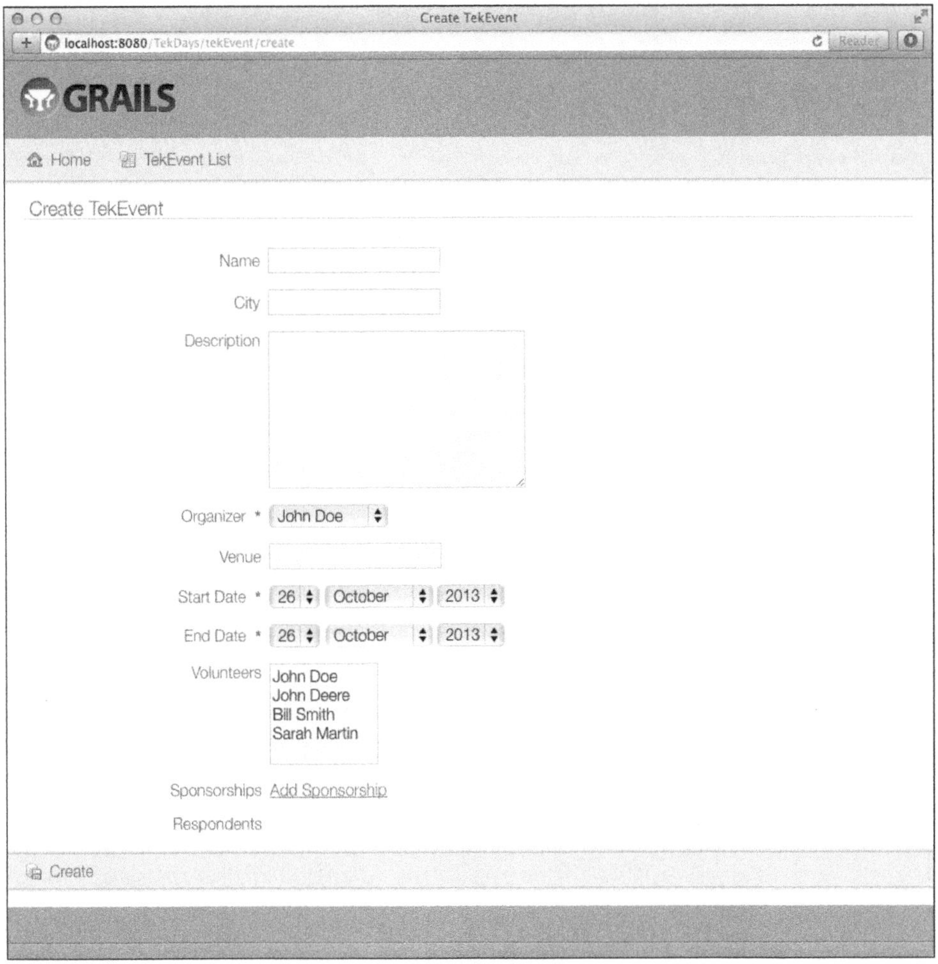

Figure 22—**TekEvent** create view

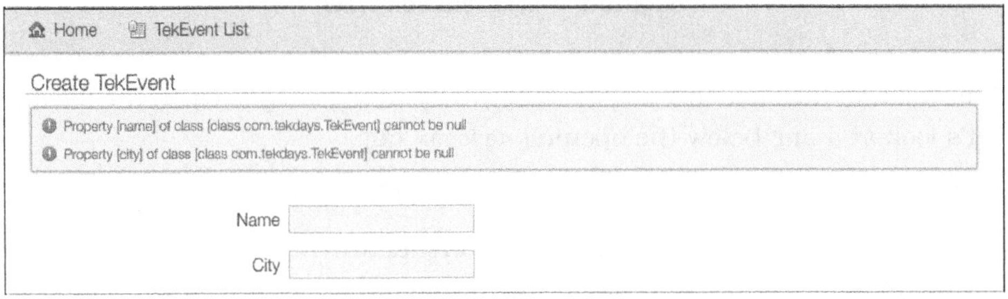

Figure 23—**Built-in error handling**

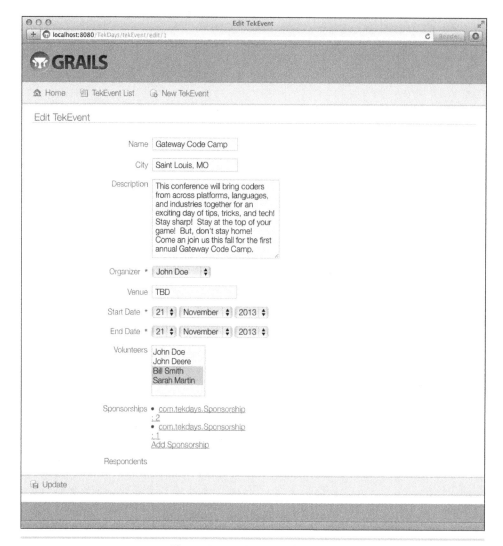

Figure 24—TekEvent edit view

You will find the code in TekDays/grails-app/views/tekEvent/edit.gsp. Open the file and let's look at a line below the opening <g:form> tag:

```
<g:hiddenField name="version" value="${tekEventInstance?.version}" />
```

Here we see <g:hiddenField> being used to create an HTML <input type="hidden"> for the version of the tekEvenInstance. This is, of course, unique to the edit view, because it submits to the update action of the TekEventController, which is dealing with an existing TekEvent instance. That action will check version before we update the instance to avoid conflicts with changes by another user.

The form Template

The main body of both the create and edit views is in the form template, which is located in TekDays/grails-app/views/tekEvent/_form.gsp. Open this file, and let's see what new and exciting things it has in store for us:

```
<div class="fieldcontain ${hasErrors(bean: tekEventInstance, field: 'name',
  'error')} ">
  <label for="name">
    <g:message code="tekEvent.name.label" default="Name" />
  </label>
  <g:textField name="name" value="${tekEventInstance?.name}"/>
</div>
```

The create and edit views use a two-column layout similar to that of the show view. The difference is that where the show view uses an ordered list to display our event's properties, this template has a <div> for each property, containing HTML input elements. <g:textField>, for example, is a GSP tag that renders an HTML text input field with the specified name and value attributes. Notice how the <g:hasErrors> tag is used in a Groovy expression to determine whether to use the error CSS class. That doesn't look like a tag, does it? As we saw in *The Save Action*, on page 63, all GSP tags can also be called as methods. How's that for versatile?

```
<div class="fieldcontain ${hasErrors(bean: tekEventInstance, field: 'description',
  'error')} ">
  <label for="description">
    <g:message code="tekEvent.description.label" default="Description" />
  </label>
  <g:textArea name="description" cols="40" rows="5" maxlength="5000"
    value="${tekEventInstance?.description}"/>
</div>
```

For the description property, Grails is using <g:textArea>, a GSP tag which (unsurprisingly enough) renders a <textarea> element.

```
<div class="fieldcontain ${hasErrors(bean: tekEventInstance, field: 'organizer',
  'error')} required">
  <label for="organizer">
    <g:message code="tekEvent.organizer.label" default="Organizer" />
    <span class="required-indicator">*</span>
  </label>
  <g:select id="organizer" name="organizer.id" from="${com.tekdays.TekUser.list()}"
    optionKey="id" required="" value="${tekEventInstance?.organizer?.id}"
    class="many-to-one"/>
</div>
```

For properties that are references to another domain class, Grails uses a <g:select> tag, which will render a <select> element loaded with all the available choices for that class. In this case, we end up with a list of TekUser instances that can be assigned to the organizer property.

```
<div class="fieldcontain ${hasErrors(bean: tekEventInstance, field: 'startDate',
  'error')} required">
  <label for="startDate">
    <g:message code="tekEvent.startDate.label" default="Start Date" />
    <span class="required-indicator">*</span>
  </label>
  <g:datePicker name="startDate" precision="day"
    value="${tekEventInstance?.startDate}"  />
</div>
```

The <g:datePicker> tag renders that series of select elements that we see in Figure 22, *TekEvent create view*, on page 75. Grails is using the tag's precision attribute to indicate that we only want to specify a particular day (by default, the tag will render select elements for all of year, month, day, hour, and minute). Another useful attribute of this tag (not used here) is noSelection.[18]

```
<div class="fieldcontain ${hasErrors(bean: tekEventInstance, field:
  'volunteers', 'error')} ">
  <label for="volunteers">
    <g:message code="tekEvent.volunteers.label" default="Volunteers" />

  </label>
  <g:select name="volunteers" from="${com.tekdays.TekUser.list()}"
    multiple="multiple" optionKey="id" size="5"
    value="${tekEventInstance?.volunteers*.id}" class="many-to-many"/>
</div>
```

Grails also uses a <g:select> tag for unidirectional one-to-many relationships. In this case, the multiple attribute is set, and the value attribute is set to the id of each TekUser instance in the volunteers collection property, using Groovy's *spread operator*.[19] This will render a multiselect listbox loaded with TekUser instances. When submitted, all the selected instances will be automagically added to the volunteers property.

```
<div class="fieldcontain ${hasErrors(bean: tekEventInstance, field: 'sponsorships',
  'error')} ">
  <label for="sponsorships">
    <g:message code="tekEvent.sponsorships.label" default="Sponsorships" />
  </label>

<ul class="one-to-many">
<g:each in="${tekEventInstance?.sponsorships?}" var="s">
  <li><g:link controller="sponsorship" action="show"
```

---

18. See http://grails.org/doc/2.3.1/ref/Tags/datePicker.html.

19. See http://mrhaki.blogspot.com/2009/08/groovy-goodness-spread-dot-operator.html.

```
        id="${s.id}">${s?.encodeAsHTML()}</g:link></li>
</g:each>
<li class="add">
<g:link controller="sponsorship" action="create" params="['tekEvent.id':
  tekEventInstance?.id]">${message(code: 'default.add.label',
  args: [message(code: 'sponsorship.label', default: 'Sponsorship')])}</g:link>
</li>
</ul>

</div>
```

In this block, we can see how the sponsorship collection property is rendered as an unordered list of links. A <g:each> tag creates a <li> for each sponsorship, and after it is closed, we have one last <li>, containing a <g:link> tag that will render a link to the create action of the SponsorshipController. The value in the params attribute will cause this TekEvent instance to be assigned to the tekEvent property of the newly-created Sponsorship.

And this concludes our tour of the code behind the scaffolded views. Now that this code is available to us and we have a working understanding of what it is doing, we can see how we could make a few changes to make our application a little better looking and easier to use. We'll do that beginning in the next chapter, but first, let's see how we can hook up to a real database so we no longer lose our data changes every time we restart the application.

Configuring a Database

The in-memory database that comes with Grails is handy, and we have been making good use of it, but a time comes in the life of any application when you need to store your data in a real database. (Let's hope this happens before you go to production.) As with most things, Grails makes this a snap to do.

"Configuration?" You may be wondering what happened to "convention over configuration." Well, keep in mind that it's *over*, not *instead of*, and, besides, no matter how hard Larry Ellison tries, there's still no convention for which database to use.[20] Also, Grails takes much of the pain out of the word *configuration* by allowing us to write all of our configuration code in Groovy instead of XML. The information about our database is in TekDays/grails-app/conf/DataSource.groovy. By default, it looks like this:

```
dataSource {
    pooled = true
    driverClassName = "org.h2.Driver"
```

---

20. Larry Ellison is the cofounder and CEO of Oracle, maker of the leading enterprise database. See http://en.wikipedia.org/wiki/Larry_Ellison.

```
        username = "sa"
        password = ""
}
hibernate {
    cache.use_second_level_cache = true
    cache.use_query_cache = false
    cache.region.factory_class =
      'net.sf.ehcache.hibernate.EhCacheRegionFactory' // Hibernate 3
//    cache.region.factory_class =
//        'org.hibernate.cache.ehcache.EhCacheRegionFactory' // Hibernate 4
}
// environment specific settings
environments {
    development {
        dataSource {
            dbCreate = "create-drop" // one of 'create', 'create-drop',
                                     //'update', 'validate', ''
            url = "jdbc:h2:mem:devDb;MVCC=TRUE;LOCK_TIMEOUT=10000"
        }
    }
    test {
        dataSource {
            dbCreate = "update"
            url = "jdbc:h2:mem:testDb;MVCC=TRUE;LOCK_TIMEOUT=10000"
        }
    }
    production {
        dataSource {
            dbCreate = "update"
            url = "jdbc:h2:prodDb;MVCC=TRUE;LOCK_TIMEOUT=10000"
            properties {
                maxActive = -1
                minEvictableIdleTimeMillis=1800000
                timeBetweenEvictionRunsMillis=1800000
                numTestsPerEvictionRun=3
                testOnBorrow=true
                testWhileIdle=true
                testOnReturn=false
                validationQuery="SELECT 1"
                jdbcInterceptors="ConnectionState"
            }
        }
    }
}
}
```

Along with your basic database information and a bit of Hibernate-specific options, this file has three environment blocks. These can be used to configure our application to use different databases for development, test, and production. For now, we'll focus on the development environment. Open TekDays/grails-app/conf/DataSource.groovy, and change it as indicated here:

beyond.2/TekDays/grails-app/conf/DataSource.groovy

```
dataSource {
    pooled = true
➤    driverClassName = "com.mysql.jdbc.Driver"
➤    username = "dave"
➤    password = "1234"
}
hibernate {
    cache.use_second_level_cache = true
    cache.use_query_cache = false
    cache.region.factory_class =
        'net.sf.ehcache.hibernate.EhCacheRegionFactory' // Hibernate 3
//   cache.region.factory_class =
//       'org.hibernate.cache.ehcache.EhCacheRegionFactory' // Hibernate 4
}

// environment specific settings
environments {
    development {
        dataSource {
➤            dbCreate = "update" // one of 'create', 'create-drop',
➤                                // 'update', 'validate', ''
➤            url = "jdbc:mysql://localhost:3306/tekdays"
        }
    }
    test {
        dataSource {
            dbCreate = "update"
            url = "jdbc:h2:mem:testDb;MVCC=TRUE;LOCK_TIMEOUT=10000"
        }
    }
    production {
        dataSource {
            dbCreate = "update"
            url = "jdbc:h2:prodDb;MVCC=TRUE;LOCK_TIMEOUT=10000"
            properties {
                maxActive = -1
                minEvictableIdleTimeMillis=1800000
                timeBetweenEvictionRunsMillis=1800000
                numTestsPerEvictionRun=3
                testOnBorrow=true
                testWhileIdle=true
                testOnReturn=false
                validationQuery="SELECT 1"
                jdbcInterceptors="ConnectionState"
            }
        }
    }
}
```

Next we need to make a simple change to TekDays/grails-app/conf/BuildConfig.groovy. Grails includes a dependency in this file for the MySQL JDBC connector, but it's commented out by default. Open the file and uncomment the highlighted line:

beyond.2/TekDays/grails-app/conf/BuildConfig.groovy
```
dependencies {
    // specify dependencies here under either 'build', 'compile', 'runtime',
    // 'test' or 'provided' scopes e.g.
    runtime 'mysql:mysql-connector-java:5.1.24'
}
```

We also need to create an empty database called tekdays. Grails will create all the tables for us when we run the application for the first time.

One last note regarding the database: the first time we run the application with a real database, the bootstrap code will execute and create some initial data for us. Unless we remove it or code around it, this will happen *every time* we run the application. So, before we end up with a ton of duplicate data, it's a good idea to remove the bootstrap code after it has been run once or add code to ensure it will run only once. For example, we could wrap the code in Bootstrap.init() with an if block, like this:

```
if (!TekEvent.get(1)){
  //bootstrap code goes here...
}
```

With this code in place, the entire init block will be ignored after the first time it is run. To help with making changes once an application is in production, there are plugins available that enable database migrations.[21]

Before we leave this topic, here's another strategy. Some choose to leave the development database as an H2 in-memory database and provide persistent databases for test and production. In this case, we would make the bootstrap code conditional on environment instead of data. Here's an example of how to do this:

```
import grails.util.GrailsUtil
...
if (GrailsUtil.environment == 'development'){
  //bootstrap code goes here...
}
```

---

21. The Grails Database Migration plugin (which, as we saw, is installed by default in Grails) is one example of such a plugin. See http://grails.org/plugin/database-migration.

Summary

Our application is actually in roughly the same state as it was at the beginning of this chapter, but now we've armed ourselves with the knowledge and the code necessary to begin making major progress. In the next chapter, we will deal with some of the UI issues that were bothering our customer, and then we'll tackle the next feature on our list.

CHAPTER 6

Getting Things Done

In this iteration, we're going to take advantage of the generated scaffolding code to make our views more pleasing to our customer. We'll also work on implementing the task list features of TekDays so that TekDays users can get things done. Along the way, we'll learn just how easy it is to modify and extend Grails views.

Changing All Our Views at Once

We saw in the previous chapter how Grails uses SiteMesh to provide a consistent look throughout an application. That's what's been giving us that cool Grails logo on all of our views. But that's not quite what our customer wants for TekDays. Let's see what we can do about that. Open TekDays/grails-app/views/layout/main.gsp, and in the <body> section, modify the first <div>:

things.2/TekDays/grails-app/views/layouts/main.gsp
```
<div id="logo" role="banner"><a href="${createLink(uri: '/')}">
  <img src="${resource(dir: 'images', file: 'td_logo.png')}"
    alt="TekDays"/></a></div>
```

We renamed the <div>, changed the link to point to the TekDays home page, and replaced the logo. Of course, you can substitute your own logo design, or you can download td_logo from the book's website. Talk about low-hanging fruit! Our new logo will now show up on every page of our application. In Figure 25, *TekDays home page with new logo*, on page 86, we get a peek at what our pages will look like.

That's not all we can do in this file, but it's all we need to do for now. We could go on and add sidebars, a footer, a standard menu, and so on. But we don't want to get ahead of ourselves.

Let's look at another file that is shared across all the views in our application. Grails puts the CSS code for the scaffolded views in web-app/css/main.css. We can

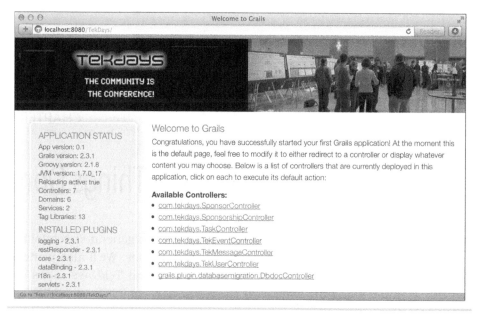

Figure 25—TekDays home page with new logo

change many aspects of our views by modifying this file. In an effort to keep style code out of our pages, we will be adding to this file for the small amount of additional CSS that we will be using in TekDays. The additional style rules that we are using can be found in Appendix 1, *Additional CSS Rules*, on page 179. Now let's turn our attention to our scaffolded views.

Modifying the Scaffolded Views

We're going to go through the scaffolded view code of the TekEvent class and make some simple modifications. (The things we change here can just as easily be done for the other classes' views.) As we go through these changes, we can leave the application running and immediately see the changes by simply refreshing the browser—another example of how Grails keeps that rapid feedback loop going. This also takes the pain out of the tweaking process that we so often have to go through to get a page "just right."

The List View

We'll start by removing the organizer from the list view. When we generated the scaffolded views, Grails simply used the first six properties of our TekEvent for the table in the list view, and this included organizer. But the organizer is not really something users will be concerned with as they look through a list of events.

Let's see what this looks like. Open TekDays/grails-app/views/tekEvent/index.gsp, and go to the <thead> block. Remove the Organizer column. You should be left with this:

```
<thead>
    <tr>
      <g:sortableColumn property="name"
        title="${message(code: 'tekEvent.name.label',
        default: 'Name')}" />
      <g:sortableColumn property="city"
        title="${message(code: 'tekEvent.city.label',
        default: 'City')}" />
      <g:sortableColumn property="description"
        title="${message(code: 'tekEvent.description.label',
        default: 'Description')}" />
      <g:sortableColumn property="venue"
        title="${message(code: 'tekEvent.venue.label',
        default: 'Venue')}" />
      <g:sortableColumn property="startDate"
        title="${message(code: 'tekEvent.startDate.label',
        default: 'Start Date')}" />
    </tr>
</thead>
```

Next, remove the associated <td> from the <tbody>. It should look like this:

```
<tbody>
<g:each in="${tekEventInstanceList}" status="i"
  var="tekEventInstance">
  <tr class="${(i % 2) == 0 ? 'even' : 'odd'}">
    <td><g:link action="show"
      id="${tekEventInstance.id}">
      ${fieldValue(bean: tekEventInstance,
        field: "name")}</g:link>
    </td>
    <td>${fieldValue(bean: tekEventInstance,
      field: "city")}</td>
    <td>${fieldValue(bean: tekEventInstance,
      field: "description")}
    </td>
    <td>${fieldValue(bean: tekEventInstance,
      field: "venue")}</td>
    <td><g:formatDate
      date="${tekEventInstance.startDate}" />
    </td>
  </tr>
</g:each>
</tbody>
```

Now when we refresh the page, it will look like the following figure.

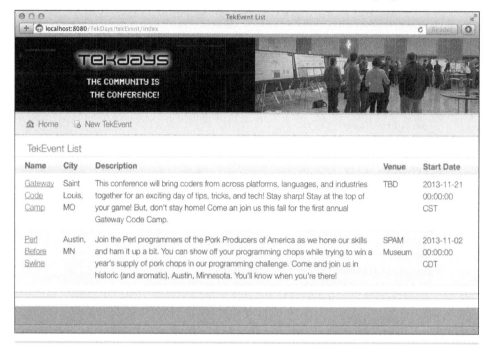

Figure 26—Modified **TekEvent** list view

The Show View

The show view presents several opportunities for improvement. We'll go through from top to bottom and fix things up. You can save the file and refresh after each step, and we'll show the new view when we're done. Open TekDays/grails-app/views/tekEvent/show.gsp, and let's get started.

Near the top of this file you'll see an <h1> containing a <g:message> tag that will render the text "Show TekEvent." Let's replace that tag with the name of the event:

```
things.2/TekDays/grails-app/views/tekEvent/show.gsp
<h1>${tekEventInstance?.name}</h1>
```

This is an example of how we can use Groovy expressions anywhere on a page.

Next, let's remove the name property from the main part of the page, because we already have it displayed in the heading. Notice that each property is displayed within a <li> tag surrounded by <g:if> tags; just remove the opening

<g:if>, the closing </g:if>, and everything in between. You can repeat this process for any other properties you want to remove.

We'll move description to right above city. We'll move the organizer down directly before the volunteers. Then we'll do something a little more clever for the city property:

```
things.2/TekDays/grails-app/views/tekEvent/show.gsp
<g:if test="${tekEventInstance?.city}">
<li class="fieldcontain">
➤   <span id="city-label" class="property-label">
➤     Location
➤   </span>

    <span class="property-value" aria-labelledby="city-label">
➤     <g:fieldValue bean="${tekEventInstance}" field="venue"/>,
➤     <g:fieldValue bean="${tekEventInstance}" field="city"/>
    </span>

</li>
</g:if>
```

We changed the label, which is the value in the first <span>, to "Location," and we included the venue in the same line.

Next we'll tackle the date properties. The way they're currently being displayed is not going to cut it. Sure, people will want their events to run on schedule, but they're probably not going to worry about the exact hour, minute, and second that it starts.

```
things.2/TekDays/grails-app/views/tekEvent/show.gsp
<g:if test="${tekEventInstance?.startDate}">
<li class="fieldcontain">
  <span id="startDate-label" class="property-label"><g:message
    code="tekEvent.startDate.label" default="Start Date" /></span>

  <span class="property-value" aria-labelledby="startDate-label">
➤   <g:formatDate format="MMMM dd, yyyy"
➤     date="${tekEventInstance?.startDate}" /></span>

</li>
</g:if>
```

Here we added the format attribute[1] to the <g:formatDate> tag used for startDate. Do the same with the endDate property.

---

1.   See http://docs.oracle.com/javase/6/docs/api/java/text/SimpleDateFormat.html.

```
things.2/TekDays/grails-app/views/tekEvent/show.gsp
<g:if test="${tekEventInstance?.endDate}">
<li class="fieldcontain">
  <span id="endDate-label" class="property-label"><g:message
    code="tekEvent.endDate.label" default="End Date" /></span>

  <span class="property-value" aria-labelledby="endDate-label">
    <g:formatDate format="MMMM dd, yyyy"
      date="${tekEventInstance?.endDate}" /></span>

</li>
</g:if>
```

Finally, let's clean up the way the Sponsorship collection is displayed. Recall from the discussion in *Many-to-Many Relationships*, on page 49, that we did not declare a toString() method because the way we display a Sponsorship will depend on the context. That's why it currently shows up as com.tekdays.Sponsorship : 1. Since we're working on the TekEvent views, we'll modify the display with that context in mind.

```
things.2/TekDays/grails-app/views/tekEvent/show.gsp
<g:if test="${tekEventInstance?.sponsorships}">
<li class="fieldcontain">
  <span id="sponsorships-label" class="property-label"><g:message
    code="tekEvent.sponsorships.label" default="Sponsorships" /></span>

  <g:each in="${tekEventInstance.sponsorships}" var="s">
  <span class="property-value" aria-labelledby="sponsorships-label">
    <g:link controller="sponsorship" action="show"
      id="${s.id}">${s?.sponsor.encodeAsHTML()}</g:link></span>
  </g:each>

</li>
</g:if>
```

All we had to do was change the s?.encodeAsHTML() to s?.sponsor.encodeAsHTML(). If this was the Sponsor show view, we would change it to s?.event.encodeAsHTML(). Take a look at Figure 27, *Modified TekEvent show view*, on page 91 to see the results of our changes.

The Create and Edit Views

As we discussed in Chapter 5, *Beyond Scaffolding*, on page 59, the create and edit views share the form elements contained in the _form.gsp template. For our purposes, this template doesn't need too much work. One thing we can do is fix the date ranges that we accept. Open TekDays/grails-

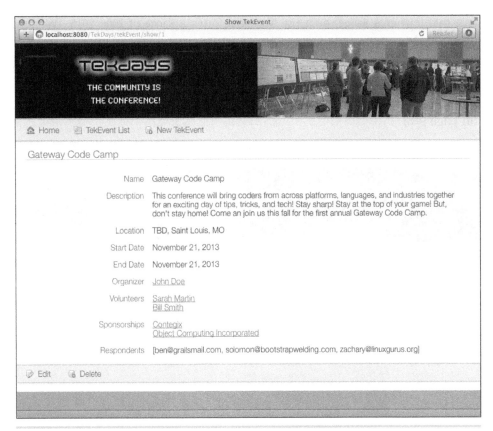

Figure 27—Modified TekEvent show view

app/views/tekEvent/_form.gsp, and zero in on the <g:datePicker> tag used for the startDate property.

```
things.2/TekDays/grails-app/views/tekEvent/_form.gsp
<div class="fieldcontain ${hasErrors(bean: tekEventInstance,
  field: 'startDate',
  'error')} required">
      <label for="startDate">
            <g:message code="tekEvent.startDate.label" default="Start Date" />
            <span class="required-indicator">*</span>
      </label>
      <g:datePicker name="startDate" precision="day"
   value="${tekEventInstance?.startDate}" years="${2008..2015}" />
</div>
```

The <g:datePicker> tag can take a years attribute, which will allow us to limit the years from which a user can pick. (Without this attribute, the tag will just list every year for 100 years before and after the current year.) This attribute can take either a Range[2] or a List. We gave ours a Range of 2008..2015. (We can also add this attribute to the endDate <g:datePicker> tag.)

Now, because both of these views are constructed using the same template that we've been working on, we can refresh either of these views and see the result! (See the following figure and Figure 29, *Modified TekEvent edit view*, on page 93.)

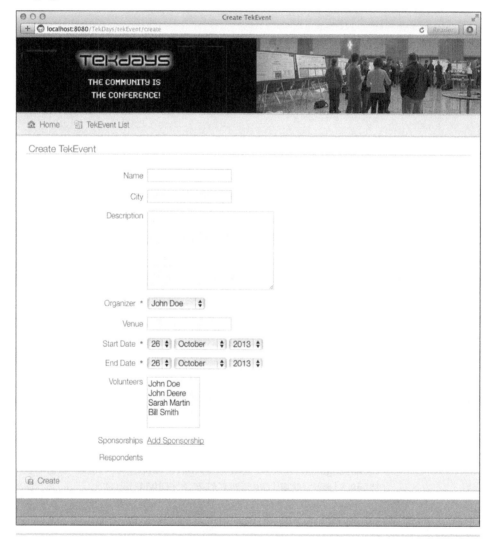

Figure 28—Modified **TekEvent** create view

---

2.   See http://groovy.codehaus.org/Collections.

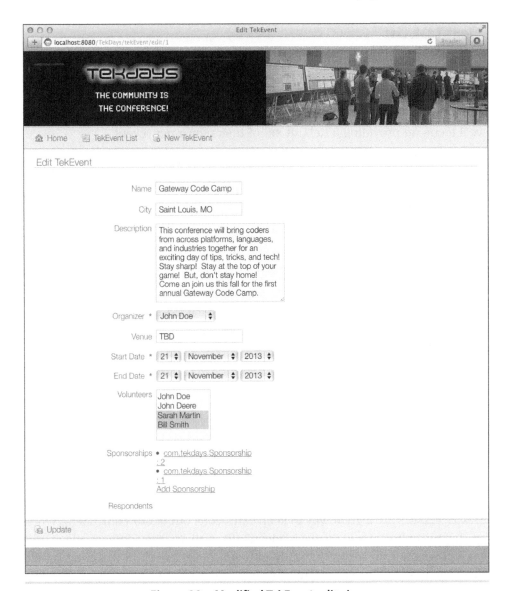

Figure 29—Modified TekEvent edit view

We may return to some of these views later, but for now things are looking much nicer. Now that *we've* gotten some things done, we'll move on to the next feature in our list. We'll add a task list to our application so that our *users* can get things done.

Event Task List

According to our feature list, we need to be able to add and remove tasks, assign tasks, and have a default set of tasks. We already have the add and remove bit done: we have the same four scaffolded views for the Task that we have for the TekEvent. They were created when we ran the generate-all script. So, we'll focus on providing a default set of tasks for a new event.

The task list feature will enable users to keep track of the many things that need to be done to put on a successful technical conference. Tasks will be assigned to volunteers, but the list will be available to the whole team. It's important to keep an eye on those details, or they'll fall through the cracks. According to our customer, most of the users will not have experience organizing an event of this magnitude. The idea behind the default tasks, then, is to give them some ideas and a starting point.

Our customer has provided us with a set of default tasks. Rather than listing them here, we'll practice the DRY principle.[3] We'll list the default tasks in the code that we write to create them. Now we need to figure out where to put that code.

Grails Service Classes

We're going to write a method that will create several Task instances and add them to the tasks property of a newly created TekEvent. We will define this method in a *service* class. A Grails service class is a Plain Old Groovy Object (POGO) located in the grails-app/services directory and with a name ending in *Service*. By following these conventions, this plain old Groovy object will be endowed with magical powers.

Service classes are a great way to keep extra code out of our controllers. When we have application logic that doesn't fit well in any domain class—for example, logic that involves multiple domain classes—it is tempting to add this code to the controller. Doing this can lead to bloated controllers that are difficult to read and maintain. To keep our controller leaner, we can move this type of application logic into service methods. We can't give a full treatment of service classes here, but we'll discuss some of their features as we put them to use.[4] Grails provides a convenience script to create a new service class. Let's try it:

---

3. DRY stands for Don't Repeat Yourself. This is one of the core principles in *The Pragmatic Programmer [HT00]*.

4. You can find more details on Grails service classes at http://grails.org/doc/2.3.1/guide/services.html.

```
$ grails create-service com.tekdays.Task
```

We called our service TaskService because we're going to use it to create Task instances. Before we get started with that, let's take a look at what Grails created for us:

things.2/TekDays/grails-app/services/com/tekdays/TaskService.groovy
```
package com.tekdays

import grails.transaction.Transactional

class TaskService {

    def serviceMethod() {

    }
}
```

We start with a stubbed-out method called serviceMethod(), which by default will be executed in a transaction.[5] This is because, by default, any method declared in a service class in Grails will be executed within a transaction.[6] We don't have to do anything to enable transactions; everything is handled behind the scenes by Spring and Hibernate. If you've ever had to code transaction handling in a web application, we'll give you a moment to get your jaw off the floor.

Now let's add a method to TaskService called addDefaultTasks(tekEvent). Open TekDays/grails-app/services/com/tekdays/TaskService.groovy, and add the following code:

things.2/TekDays/grails-app/services/com/tekdays/TaskService.groovy
```
def addDefaultTasks(tekEvent){
    if (tekEvent.tasks?.size() > 0)
        return //We only want to add tasks to a new event

    tekEvent.addToTasks new Task(title:'Identify potential venues')
    tekEvent.addToTasks new Task(title:'Get price / availability of venues')
    tekEvent.addToTasks new Task(title:'Compile potential sponsor list')
    tekEvent.addToTasks new Task(title:'Design promotional materials')
    tekEvent.addToTasks new Task(title:'Compile potential advertising avenues')
    tekEvent.addToTasks new Task(title:'Locate swag provider (preferably local)')
    tekEvent.save()
}
```

---

5. See http://en.wikipedia.org/wiki/Database_transaction.
6. If you're creating a read-only service, or one that doesn't use the database at all, you can disable this by setting the transactional property to false. See http://grails.org/doc/2.3.1/guide/services.html#declarativeTransactions.

Let's walk through this code. First, we check to see whether the tekEvent passed in has anything in its tasks collection. If it does, then we bail. Otherwise, we begin a series of calls to tekEvent.addToTasks(). This method is one of the many added dynamically by Grails. (Notice that we're taking advantage of Groovy's optional parentheses to reduce the noise in our code.) Finally, we call tekEvent.save(), which will cascade to save all the Task instances too.

That's it for our service class, but now we need to use it. The logical place to do that would be in the save action of the TekEventController; that way, we can be sure that the default tasks will be added to every TekEvent that is successfully saved. Open TekDays/grails-app/controllers/com/tekdays/TekEventController.groovy, and add this single property declaration at the top of the class:

```
things.2/TekDays/grails-app/controllers/com/tekdays/TekEventController.groovy
package com.tekdays

import static org.springframework.http.HttpStatus.*
import grails.transaction.Transactional

@Transactional(readOnly = true)
class TekEventController {

    def taskService
    static allowedMethods = [save: "POST", update: "PUT", delete: "DELETE"]

    def index(Integer max) {
        params.max = Math.min(max ?: 10, 100)
        respond TekEvent.list(params),
          model:[tekEventInstanceCount: TekEvent.count()]
    }
```

All we have to do is to declare a property named after the service class (with the first letter lowercase), and an instance of that class will be injected into our controller at runtime. That's *autowiring* Grails style, and it's pretty awesome! We don't need to create an instance of TaskService and assign it to our controller, and we don't need to worry about ensuring that it exists before we call it. It's all managed for us by Grails, courtesy of "convention over configuration."

Now in the save action, we'll add the call to addDefaultTasks():

```
things.2/TekDays/grails-app/controllers/com/tekdays/TekEventController.groovy
@Transactional
def save(TekEvent tekEventInstance) {
    if (tekEventInstance == null) {
        notFound()
        return
    }
```

```
    if (tekEventInstance.hasErrors()) {
        respond tekEventInstance.errors, view:'create'
        return
    }
    tekEventInstance.save flush:true
➤   taskService.addDefaultTasks(tekEventInstance)

    request.withFormat {
        form {
            flash.message = message(code: 'default.created.message',
              args: [message(code: 'tekEventInstance.label',
              default: 'TekEvent'), tekEventInstance.id])
            redirect tekEventInstance
        }
        '*' { respond tekEventInstance, [status: CREATED] }
    }
}
```

We put the call after the error checking and saving of the TekEvent, so we don't waste effort trying to add tasks to a TekEvent that won't save. If it does save successfully, we'll see the default tasks loaded.

Before we test this, let's add an <li> for the tasks collection to the TekEvent show view. For this, we can just copy the "Sponsorships" <li> and modify it to display the list of tasks. Open TekDays/grails-app/views/tekEvent/show.gsp and add the following code right below the respondents <li>:

```
things.2/TekDays/grails-app/views/tekEvent/show.gsp
<g:if test="${tekEventInstance?.tasks}">
<li class="fieldcontain">
  <span id="tasks-label" class="property-label"><g:message
    code="tekEvent.tasks.label" default="Tasks" /></span>
    <g:each in="${tekEventInstance.tasks}" var="t">
    <span class="property-value" aria-labelledby="tasks-label">
      <g:link controller="task" action="show"
        id="${t.id}">${t.title}</g:link></span>
    </g:each>
</li>
</g:if>
```

And now, when we create a new event, we should see something like Figure 30, *TekEvent show view with default tasks*, on page 98.

Before we move on from here, let's write a test for our new service class. Grails has already created a stubbed-out test class for us in TekDays/test/unit/com/tek-days/TaskServiceSpec.groovy, but as we can see from the directory it's put in, this is a *unit* test. For testing our service class, we are going to use an *integration test*.

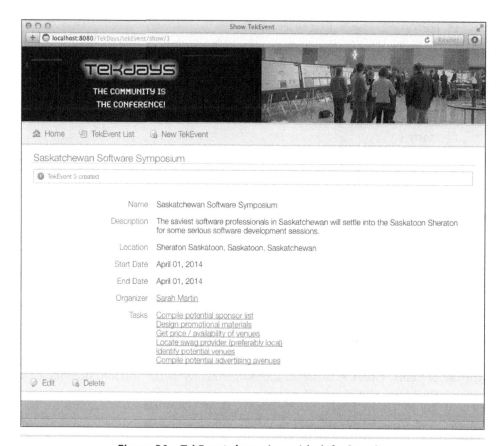

Figure 30—TekEvent show view with default tasks

Integration Testing

We create an integration test by running the Grails script create-integration-test. An integration test is a Spock specification or JUnit test case, just like a Grails unit test. The difference is in what is available to the test at runtime. Unit tests are meant to test a unit (class) in isolation, so Grails doesn't give unit tests any of its dynamic goodness. Integration tests are meant to test multiple classes working together. When running integration tests, Grails adds all of the dynamic behavior that we're taking advantage of in our application.

Since the process of adding default tasks to an event involves the TaskService, Task, and TekEvent classes, an integration test is a good fit. Run the create-integration-test script:

```
$ grails create-integration-test com.tekdays.TaskService
```

Now open TekDays/test/integration/com/tekdays/TaskServiceSpec.groovy, and add the following code:

```
things.2/TekDays/test/integration/com/tekdays/TaskServiceSpec.groovy
package com.tekdays

import grails.test.mixin.TestFor
import spock.lang.Specification

/**
 * See the API for {@link grails.test.mixin.services.ServiceUnitTestMixin}
 * for usage instructions
 */
@TestFor(TaskService)
class TaskServiceSpec extends Specification {
  def taskService

    def setup() {
      new TekUser(fullName:'Tammy Tester', userName:'tester' ,
          email:'tester@test.com' , website:'test.com' ,
          bio:'A test person').save()

    }

    def cleanup() {
    }

    void "test addDefaultTasks"() {
      when: "we pass an event to taskService.addDefaultTasks"
      def e = new TekEvent(name:'Test Event',
                city:'TestCity, USA',
                description:'Test Description',
                organizer:TekUser.findByUserName('tester' ),
                venue:'TestCenter' ,
                startDate:new Date(),
                endDate:new Date() + 1)
      taskService.addDefaultTasks(e)
    then: "the event will have 6 default tasks"
      e.tasks.size() == 6
    }
}
```

Test Data Source

Integration tests will use the data source for the *test* environment. Before running integration tests, you may want to set the data source for this environment to a persistent database. For an example, refer to *Configuring a Database*, on page 79.

At the top of this file, we declare a taskService property, just like we did in the TekEventController. Then in the setup() method, we create and save a TekUser. We have to do this because the organizer property of TekEvent does not accept nulls; we need a real TekUser to assign to that property. Then, in the "test addDefault-Tasks"() method (the test), we're creating a TekEvent and passing it to the taskService.addDefaultTasks() method. Finally, we state that our event's tasks property contains the number of items that our service method is adding.

If you've been adding valid tests for our artifacts as we've gone along, you can run them now with grails test-app, and you should see them all pass. That's a good feeling!

Modifying the Task Class

Great! We now have default tasks on all new events, users can add and remove tasks as needed, and tasks can be assigned to users. But there's something missing....

Excuse us while we take off our customer hats and smack ourselves in the forehead.

We don't have any way to mark a task as completed! Not to worry—we'll just do a quick bit of reworking, and we'll be good to go. First we'll modify the Task class. Open TekDays/grails-app/domain/com/tekdays/Task.groovy, and add a new property and constraint, as shown here:

```
things.2/TekDays/grails-app/domain/com/tekdays/Task.groovy
package com.tekdays

class Task {
    String title
    String notes
    TekUser assignedTo
    Date dueDate
    TekEvent event
➤   Boolean completed

    static constraints = {
        title blank: false
        notes blank: true, nullable: true, maxSize: 5000
        assignedTo nullable: true
        dueDate nullable: true
➤       completed nullable: true
    }

    static belongsTo = TekEvent
}
```

Now that we have a completed property to work with, let's modify our views to take advantage of it. Open TekDays/grails-app/views/task/show.gsp, and add an <li> block at the bottom of the <ol>, like so:

```
things.2/TekDays/grails-app/views/task/show.gsp
  <g:if test="${taskInstance?.completed}">
  <li class="fieldcontain">
    <span id="completed-label" class="property-label"><g:message
      code="task.completed.label" default="Completed" /></span>

      <span class="property-value" aria-labelledby="completed-label">
        <g:formatBoolean boolean="${taskInstance?.completed}"
          true="Yes" false="No" /></span>

  </li>
  </g:if>

</ol>
```

We're using the <g:formatBoolean> tag, which will render the text we give it for either its true or false attributes depending on the value of the property. This will allow our users to see when a Task is completed.

Next, open TekDays/grails-app/views/task/_form.gsp, and add the following <div> at the end:

```
things.2/TekDays/grails-app/views/task/_form.gsp
<div class="fieldcontain ${hasErrors(bean: taskInstance, field: 'completed',
  'error')} ">
  <label for="completed">
    <g:message code="task.completed.label" default="Completed" />

  </label>
  <g:checkBox name="completed" value="${taskInstance?.completed}" />
</div>
```

This will add a checkbox to our edit view so that users can mark a task as completed. (See Figure 31, *Task edit view*, on page 102.)

Summary

Well, this was a productive iteration. We implemented our task-related features, and along the way, we learned about Grails service classes, integration testing, and what it takes to modify or extend a Grails domain class after we've generated the code. Take a break. You deserve it! Catch up on some blogs (http://groovyblogs.org would be a good choice) or email. Next we will work on adding a message forum and see what we can learn while we're at it.

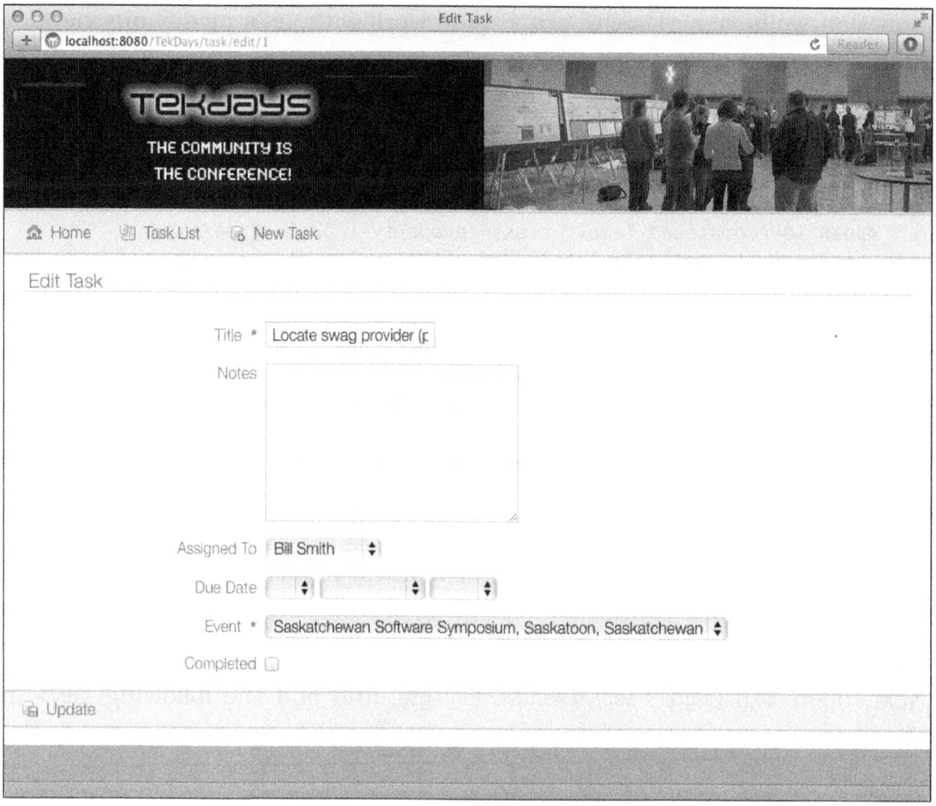

Figure 31—Task edit view

CHAPTER 7

Forum Messages and UI Tricks

A technical event, like any collaborative project, will turn out better if the communication flows freely. To help facilitate this for our users, we're going to include a forum where the organizer and volunteers can post and reply to messages. Then, to make it easy for new volunteers to come up to speed on what's going on, we'll include a threaded view of all past messages. That's the goal of this iteration. While we're at it, we'll learn more about the interaction between controllers and views, we'll get a closer look at GSP templates, and we'll get a look at Ajax, Grails style.

We won't have to start from scratch, because Grails has already given us the list, create, show, and edit views to work with. The create view (see Figure 32, *Scaffolded create view*, on page 104), for example, gives us everything we need to create a new message.

We need to change a few things to turn these scaffolded pages into a usable message forum. Our users should be able to see messages in a more logical manner than a plain list. They'll also need the ability to reply to a message they are reading, preferably without leaving the page.

Restricting Messages to an Event

Since we want the messages to constitute a forum for a given event, we'll have to modify the scaffolded views to limit the viewing and creating of TekMessage instances to the TekEvent they relate to. It's important to note that the relationship between TekEvent and TekMessage is already established in the domain model; we're just going to make the workflow match that relationship.

We'll start by modifying the event show view. We're going to add a single "Messages" hyperlink that will lead to the message list view, and we are going to filter the list to show only those TekMessage instances that are related to the TekEvent.

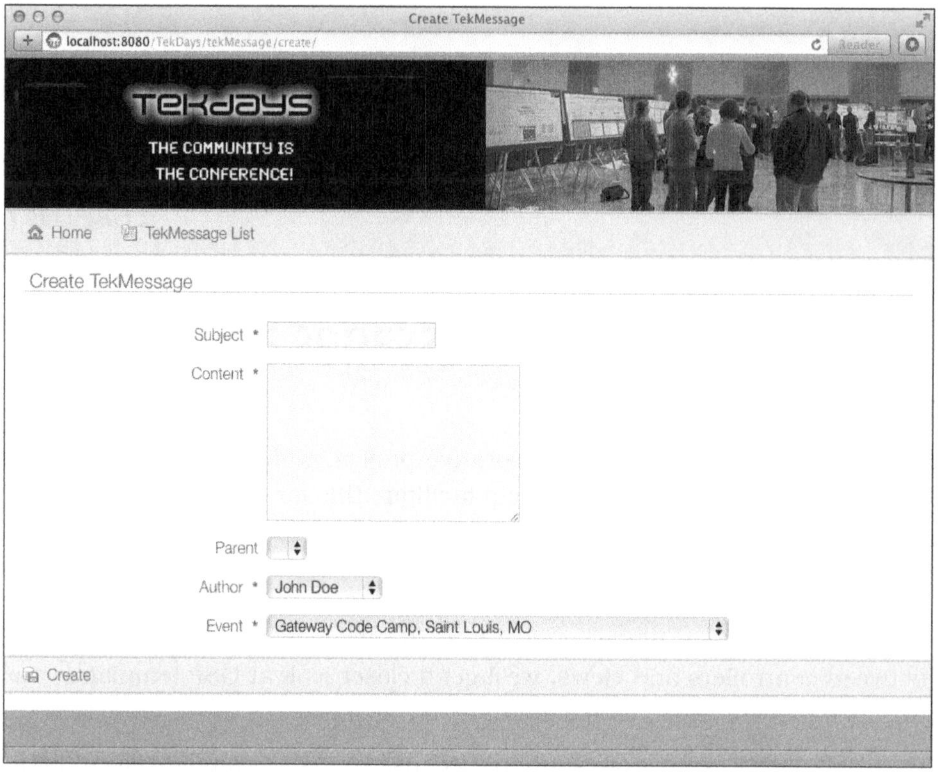

Figure 32—Scaffolded create view

Open TekDays/grails-app/views/tekEvent/show.gsp, and add the following code below
the tasks <li> that we added earlier:

forum.2/TekDays/grails-app/views/tekEvent/show.gsp
```
<g:if test="${tekEventInstance?.messages}">
<li class="fieldcontain">
  <span id="messages-label" class="property-label"><g:message
    code="tekEvent.messages.label" default="Messages" /></span>

    <span class="property-value" aria-labelledby="messages-label">
      <g:link controller="tekMessage" action="index"
        id="${tekEventInstance.id}">
        View Messages
      </g:link></span>

</li>
</g:if>
```

The <g:link> tag will create a link to the index action of the TekMessageController and will pass a TekEvent.id. If we follow this link now, Grails won't know what to do with the TekEvent.id, and we'll get an error.

To fix that, we'll modify the index action in the TekMessageController. Open TekDays/grails-app/controllers/com/tekdays/TekMessageController.groovy, and modify the index action as follows:

```
forum.2/TekDays/grails-app/controllers/com/tekdays/TekMessageController.groovy
def index(Integer max) {
    params.max = Math.min(max ?: 10, 100)
    def list
    def count
    def event = TekEvent.get(params.id)
    if(event){
        list = TekMessage.findAllByEvent(event, params)
        count = TekMessage.countByEvent(event)
    }
    else {
        list = TekMessage.list(params)
        count = TekMessage.count()
    }
    [tekMessageInstanceList: list,
     tekMessageInstanceCount: count,
     event: event]
}
```

Here we're replacing the call to respond() with a Map containing the data we'll use in the view. We first declare list and count variables for the Map. Then we declare an event variable and attempt to assign a TekEvent to it, using the id that was passed in from the link in the event show view. If a TekEvent is found, then we load the list and count variables using dynamic methods provided by GORM. If event is null, we fall back to the original means of retrieving the list and count. Finally, we assign list and count to their appropriate keys in the return Map, and we add the event:event key/value pair to the Map. This last step will make the TekEvent instance available to us in the list view.

Now we'll turn our attention to the TekMessage list view. If we navigate to this view using the link we just modified on the event show view, we'll only see messages related to a single event. That's great, but if we click the "New TekMessage" button, we'll need to explicitly choose the event on the message create view. We want that to be loaded automatically, and we can do it by modifying a single line of code. Let's open TekDays/grails-app/views/tekMessage/index.gsp and change the "New TekMessage" <g:link> tag like so:

```
forum.2/TekDays/grails-app/views/tekMessage/index.gsp
<li><g:link class="create" action="create"
  params='["event.id":"${event?.id}"]'><g:message
    code="default.new.label" args="[entityName]" /></g:link></li>
```

All we did here was add a params attribute to the <g:link> tag. This attribute is a Map containing parameters to be added to the URL created by the <g:link> tag. We then assign event.id to a key of the same name. (Since the key contains a ".", we had to put it in quotes.) This will result in a parameter like event.id=2. Grails' binding will use that to retrieve a TekEvent instance and assign it to the TekMessage.event property. All of that and more is done with the following single line:

```
respond new TekMessage(params)
```

Slick stuff!

Open TekDays/grails-app/views/tekMessage/create.gsp, and follow along as we make a few changes, starting with the "TekMessage List" button. We'll do the same thing to that button that we did to the link on the TekEvent show view.

```
forum.2/TekDays/grails-app/views/tekMessage/create.gsp
                    <li><g:link class="list" action="index"
id="${tekMessageInstance?.event?.id}"><g:message
  code="default.list.label" args="[entityName]" /></g:link></li>
```

That will ensure that we stay with this event's messages if we return to the list from here.

Now we'll add the name of the event to the page heading. Modify the <h1> tag to look like this:

```
forum.2/TekDays/grails-app/views/tekMessage/create.gsp
<h1>${tekMessageInstance?.event?.name} Forum - New Message</h1>
```

Next, open TekDays/grails-app/views/tekMessage/_form.gsp. Because we have the event name in the view and because we don't want to change the event from there, let's replace the <div> tag containing the event property with a hidden <input>. We don't need to display the event again, but we do need to have the value in the <form> so that it will be submitted when we save.

```
forum.2/TekDays/grails-app/views/tekMessage/_form.gsp
<g:hiddenField name="event.id" value="${tekMessageInstance?.event?.id}" />
```

Choosing what message you're replying to while creating the message doesn't make much sense, so let's remove that <div> tag too. In its place, we'll add a label inside a conditional block; that way, if this is a reply, we'll say so. Let's put this at the top of the page for clarity. Add the following code immediately after the import statement at the beginning of the form template:

```
forum.2/TekDays/grails-app/views/tekMessage/_form.gsp
<g:if test="${tekMessageInstance?.parent}">
  <div class="fieldcontain ${hasErrors(bean: tekMessageInstance,
    field: 'parent', 'error')} ">
    <label for="parent">
      In Reply to:

    </label>
    ${tekMessageInstance?.parent?.author}
  </div>
</g:if>
```

Here we used a <g:if> tag to prevent this from being rendered unless the tekMessageInstance has a parent property. The rest of this code just renders a label and the author of the parent TekMessage. (We won't see this feature yet since we don't yet have a way to create replies, but we'll get there soon enough.)

Finally, we'll use a little CSS to give our users more room to write their messages. Add class="messageField" to the subject <g:textField> and the content <g:textArea>, like so:

```
forum.2/TekDays/grails-app/views/tekMessage/_form.gsp
<div class="fieldcontain ${hasErrors(bean: tekMessageInstance,
  field: 'subject', 'error')} required">
  <label for="subject">
    <g:message code="tekMessage.subject.label" default="Subject" />
    <span class="required-indicator">*</span>
  </label>
  <g:textField name="subject" class="messageField" required=""
    value="${tekMessageInstance?.subject}"/>
</div>

<div class="fieldcontain ${hasErrors(bean: tekMessageInstance,
  field: 'content', 'error')} required">
  <label for="content">
    <g:message code="tekMessage.content.label" default="Content" />
    <span class="required-indicator">*</span>
  </label>
  <g:textArea name="content" class="messageField" cols="40" rows="5"
    maxlength="2000" required="" value="${tekMessageInstance?.content}"/>
</div>
```

In Figure 33, *Create view 2.0 (so to speak)*, on page 108, we see our new create view. That's much better. Next up: cleaning up the list and show views.

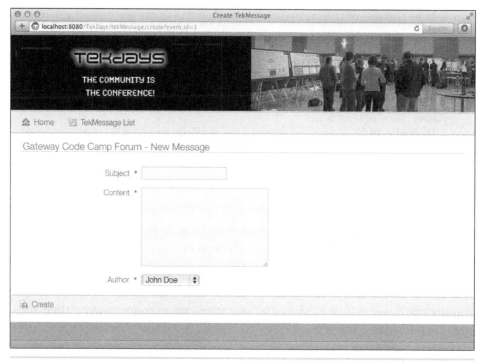

Figure 33—Create view 2.0 (so to speak)

Of Templates and Ajax

On second thought, instead of cleaning up the list and show views, let's just set them aside and create a new view that will replace them both. To do that, we'll take advantage of Grails' GSP templates.

GSP templates are simply chunks of GSP code in a file that begins with an underscore (_likethis.gsp). They provide an easy way to share common code across multiple pages (Grails' use of the _form.gsp template for our create and edit views is a great example of this). You can include a template in a GSP page with the <g:render> tag, like this:

```
<g:render template="someTemplate" />
```

This line would render a template called _someTemplate.gsp in the same directory as the page that it is being called from. To render templates from a different directory, we add the path before the name of the template. We never include the "_" at the beginning of the template name in the <g:render> tag.

Another popular use for GSP templates is rendering the response to Ajax calls; that's what we're after here. Before we get too much further, let us lay out the plan. What we want is a single page with a list of messages in the upper section, and fields for viewing a single message in the lower section. When a user selects a message in the list, that message's values will display in the fields below, without reloading the rest of the page. Pretty cool, huh? Our customer sure thought so. Now let's see how easy this can be with Grails.

To get started, let's create TekDays/grails-app/views/tekMessage/ajaxIndex.gsp. As a shortcut, just copy TekDays/grails-app/views/tekMessage/index.gsp, and remove most of it. Keep the TekMessage import statement and the <!DOCTYPE html> and <head> (with contents), and in the <body>, keep everything up to the second <div>— keep the opening and closing tags for the second <div>. You should end up with something that looks like this:

```
forum.2/TekDays/grails-app/views/tekMessage/ajaxIndex.gsp
<%@ page import="com.tekdays.TekMessage" %>
<!DOCTYPE html>
<html>
  <head>
    <meta name="layout" content="main">
    <g:set var="entityName" value="${message(code: 'tekMessage.label',
      default: 'TekMessage')}" />
    <title><g:message code="default.list.label" args="[entityName]" /></title>
  </head>
  <body>
    <a href="#list-tekMessage" class="skip" tabindex="-1"><g:message
      code="default.link.skip.label" default="Skip to content&hellip;"/></a>
    <div class="nav" role="navigation">
      <ul>
        <li><a class="home" href="${createLink(uri: '/')}"><g:message
          code="default.home.label"/></a></li>
        <li><g:link class="create" action="create"
          params='["event.id":"${event?.id}"]'><g:message
            code="default.new.label" args="[entityName]" /></g:link></li>
      </ul>
    </div>
    <div id="list-tekMessage" class="content scaffold-list" role="main">
    </div>
  </body>
</html>
```

We kept the <head> section from the list view because it contains a couple of <meta> tags that we need. Since this new view is going to replace the list view, it makes sense to keep the same button bar. Other than that, we kept only the basic page structure tags.

To flesh out the body of our new view, add the following code right after that second opening <div> tag:

```
forum.2/TekDays/grails-app/views/tekMessage/ajaxIndex.gsp
<h1>${event?.name} - Forum Messages</h1>
<div id="messageList">
  <g:each in="${tekMessageInstanceList}" var="tekMessageInstance">
  </g:each>
</div>
<h3>Message Details</h3>
<div id="details">
</div>
```

First we added an <h1> tag, similar to the one on the create view, using the
TekEvent instance that will be passed in from the controller. Then we added a
<div>, with an ID of messageList, to hold the list of messages. We have a style
rule in main.css for this ID that will provide scrolling if our list gets that long.
(See Appendix 1, *Additional CSS Rules*, on page 179.) Inside this <div>, we have
a <g:each> tag, which will iterate over the tekMessageInstanceList. Whatever we put
in the body of that tag will be displayed once for each element in the list. We'll
talk about what to put there shortly.

Below the list <div>, we added an <h3> tag to serve as a heading to the message
detail portion of the page. Finally, we added a <div> with an id of details. This
is where the message detail template that we are about to create will be rendered.

Creating the Template

Now we need to create the template that will display an individual message.
This time, just create a blank file called _details.gsp in the TekDays/grails-
app/views/tekMessage directory. We'll borrow the <div>, <ol>, and three <li> tags
from TekDays/grails-app/views/tekMessage/show.gsp. (The three <li> tags are for the
subject, content, and author properties.) Because this file's code will be inserted
into another page, it doesn't need its own <html> or <head> tags.

```
forum.2/TekDays/grails-app/views/tekMessage/_details.gsp
<div id="show-tekMessage" class="content scaffold-show" role="main">
  <ol class="property-list tekMessage">
    <g:if test="${tekMessageInstance?.subject}">
    <li class="fieldcontain">
      <span id="subject-label" class="property-label"><g:message
        code="tekMessage.subject.label" default="Subject" /></span>

        <span class="property-value" aria-labelledby="subject-label">
          <g:fieldValue bean="${tekMessageInstance}" field="subject"/></span>

    </li>
    </g:if>
```

```
<g:if test="${tekMessageInstance?.content}">
<li class="fieldcontain">
  <span id="content-label" class="property-label"><g:message
    code="tekMessage.content.label" default="Content" /></span>

    <span class="property-value" aria-labelledby="content-label">
      <g:fieldValue bean="${tekMessageInstance}" field="content"/></span>

</li>
</g:if>

<g:if test="${tekMessageInstance?.author}">
<li class="fieldcontain">
  <span id="author-label" class="property-label"><g:message
    code="tekMessage.author.label" default="Author" /></span>

    <span class="property-value" aria-labelledby="author-label">
      <g:link controller="tekUser" action="show"
        id="${tekMessageInstance?.author?.id}">
        ${tekMessageInstance?.author?.encodeAsHTML()}
      </g:link></span>

</li>
</g:if>
</ol>
<g:form>
  <fieldset class="buttons">
    <g:link class="create" action="reply"
      resource="${tekMessageInstance}">Reply</g:link>
  </fieldset>
</g:form>
</div>
```

You may have noticed that we also added a Reply "button" at the bottom of the template. What we added is actually a <g:link> that will be styled to look like a button. The <g:link> will call the reply action—which we still need to create. Don't let us forget to return to that.

Looking at the code for our template, we can see that the only data element that it will need is a TekMessage instance called (believe it or not) tekMessageInstance. This is important to note, because when a template is rendered, the data it requires needs to be passed to it. A template cannot automatically see the data elements of the page that renders it. We'll look at how to provide the data to the template in the next section as we see how to render our template in response to an Ajax call.

Ajax in Grails

Grails includes several Ajax tags, which we can use to call a controller action and update a page element with the results. That's exactly what we need to do, but before we do it, let's discuss a bit about the way that Grails Ajax tags work.

Grails supports a variety of popular JavaScript libraries with regard to its Ajax tags.[1] To use these tags, we need to tell Grails which library we are using. We do this with the <g:javascript> tag and its library attribute. This tag is placed in the <head> section of a page. Let's go back to TekDays/grails-app/views/tekMessage/ajaxIndex.gsp and add the following line to the <head>:

```
forum.2/TekDays/grails-app/views/tekMessage/ajaxIndex.gsp
<g:javascript library="jquery" />
```

Now we can use one of Grails' Ajax tags, and it will adapt to use the jQuery library.[2] The tag we're going to use is <g:remoteLink>.

Let's see how this looks in our code, and then we'll discuss what it's doing. In TekDays/grails-app/views/tekMessage/ajaxIndex.gsp, add the following highlighted code to the <g:each> body in our messageList <div>:

```
forum.2/TekDays/grails-app/views/tekMessage/ajaxIndex.gsp
<g:each in="${tekMessageInstanceList}" var="tekMessageInstance">
➤   <g:remoteLink action="showDetail" id="${tekMessageInstance?.id}"
➤     update="details">
➤     <p>${tekMessageInstance.author.fullName} - ${tekMessageInstance.subject}</p>
➤   </g:remoteLink>
  </g:each>
```

The <g:remoteLink> tag can take controller, action, and id attributes. If the controller attribute is not provided, then the controller that rendered the current page will be used by default. Since the ajaxIndex view will be rendered by the TekMessageController, we don't need to specify it here. We did give it an action attribute, which points to an action (which we will create next in the TekMessageController). Then for the id, we use the tekMessageInstance variable from the <g:each>. The final attribute that we set on the <g:remoteLink> tag is update. This attribute contains the ID of the HTML element on this page that will be updated with the result of the action—in this case, details.

---

1. See the Grails website for a list of supported libraries: http://grails.org/doc/2.3.1/guide/theWebLayer.html#ajax.
2. Grails handles any differences that might exist in the way different JavaScript libraries handle the tasks involved in the Ajax tags; the behavior of these tags is the same regardless of which of the supported libraries we use.

For the body of the <g:remoteLink>, we used the tekMessageInstance variable to build a string containing the name of the message's author and the subject of the message. We'll see how this looks shortly, but first we have to create the showDetail action. Open TekDays/grails-app/controllers/com/tekdays/TekMessageController.groovy, and add the following action:

forum.2/TekDays/grails-app/controllers/com/tekdays/TekMessageController.groovy

```groovy
def showDetail() {
    def tekMessageInstance = TekMessage.get(params.id)
    if (tekMessageInstance) {
        render(template:"details", model:[tekMessageInstance:tekMessageInstance])
    }
    else {
        render "No message found with id: ${params.id}"
    }
}
```

This action expects the params to contain an id value. The first thing we do is define a tekMessageInstance variable and retrieve a TekMessage using the id value in the params. If we have a valid instance, we call the render() method and pass it the name of a template ("details") and a model, which is a Map. The model parameter is used to provide the data that the template will need; in this case, we have only one object in the model, but we can include as many objects as our template needs. The render() method will merge our template with the data in the tekMessageInstance bean and return the results as HTML. This HTML will then replace the contents of the <div> on our page.

Now there's just one thing left to do before we can marvel at our handiwork: we need to provide a way to reach our new view. If we added an action to the TekMessageController called ajaxIndex, it would automatically render our new view, but it would just be a copy of the index action, and that wouldn't be very *DRY*. So, we'll use a different approach. The same render() method that we just used for our details template can be used to render an entire view. Let's return to the index action and modify the last line (the line that returns the Map):

forum.1.2/TekDays/grails-app/controllers/com/tekdays/TekMessageController.groovy

```groovy
def index(Integer max) {
    params.max = Math.min(max ?: 10, 100)

    def list
    def count
    def event = TekEvent.get(params.id)
    if(event){
        list = TekMessage.findAllByEvent(event, params)
        count = TekMessage.countByEvent(event)
    }
```

```
    else {
        list = TekMessage.list(params)
        count = TekMessage.count()
    }
    render view:'ajaxIndex', model:[tekMessageInstanceList: list,
                                    tekMessageInstanceCount: count,
                                    event: event]
}
```

This time, we pass a view parameter instead of a template. We set that parameter to our new page, and then we pass the existing Map as the model. Now when the index action is called (for example, when we navigate to http://localhost:8080/ TekDays/tekMessage/index), our new view will be rendered.

Wait a minute. We still need to add a reply action to the TekMessageController. OK. The reply action will be functionally similar to the create action, but unlike create, it will set the parent of the *new* TekMessage to the *current* one. Hopefully you still have TekMessageController.groovy open so you can slip in the following code:

forum.1.2/TekDays/grails-app/controllers/com/tekdays/TekMessageController.groovy
```
def reply = {
    def parent = TekMessage.get(params.id)
    def tekMessageInstance = new TekMessage(parent:parent, event:parent.event,
                                            subject:"RE: $parent.subject")
    render view:'create', model:['tekMessageInstance':tekMessageInstance]
}
```

Our reply action is in the form of a closure. In this action, we take the id parameter that is passed in on the link from the ajaxIndex view and use it to retrieve a TekMessage instance. Then we create a new TekMessage, setting its parent and subject properties based on the retrieved instance. Finally, we use the render() method to render the create view with the tekMessageInstance in the model. This will open the create view, which we will now modify to handle this new responsibility.

When the create view is rendered from the reply action, the TekMessage will have a parent assigned. We'll change our view slightly to pass along this property when the message form is submitted. Open the TekDays/grails-app/views/tekMessage/_form.gsp file, and add the highlighted code to the block right after the TekMessage import statement:

forum.1.2/TekDays/grails-app/views/tekMessage/_form.gsp
```
<g:if test="${tekMessageInstance?.parent}">
    <input type="hidden" name="parent.id"
        value="${tekMessageInstance?.parent?.id}" />
    <div class="fieldcontain ${hasErrors(bean: tekMessageInstance,
        field: 'parent', 'error')} ">
```

```
<label for="parent">
    In Reply to:

</label>
${tekMessageInstance?.parent?.author}
  </div>
</g:if>
```

Inside our parent <g:if> block, we added a hidden field to store the tekMessageInstance.parent value so that it can be passed to the save action, completing the link between a reply and its parent.

It's difficult to do justice to this functionality in print, but we'll try. In the following figure, we can see our new ajaxIndex view with a message selected, and in Figure 35, *Message create view: reply*, on page 116, we can see the result of clicking the Reply button for a message. If you've done anything like this before in another Java web framework, you're probably impressed by how easy it was to do this. We've heard that that sense of awe and amazement wears off after a while. But we're still waiting.

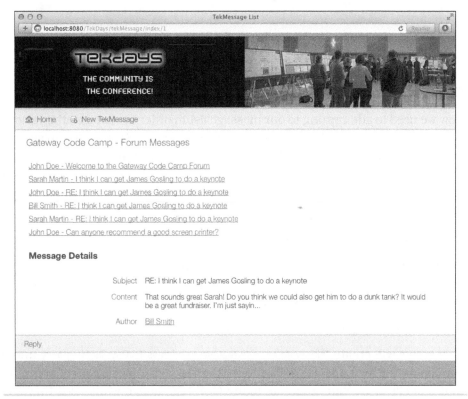

Figure 34—Ajax-enabled message list

Figure 35—Message create view: reply

Display Message Threads with a Custom Tag

Now we need to add nesting to our message list in order to visualize the various threads in our forum. We'll do this with a custom GSP tag. If you've ever written custom JSP tags or JSF components, come out from under the table. It's not like that at all. But just to reassure you, before we get started on our custom tag, we'll take a brief look at what it takes (or more important perhaps, *doesn't* take) to create a GSP tag.

A Brief Introduction to GSP Tags

The first step is to create a TagLib. A TagLib is a Groovy class with a name ending in (surprise, surprise!) TagLib, and it lives in the grails-app/taglib directory. Grails provides a convenience script to create this for us:

```
$ grails create-tag-lib com.tekdays.TekDays
```

This script will create TekDays/grails-app/taglib/com/tekdays/TekDaysTagLib.groovy and a corresponding test file in TekDays/test/unit/com/tekdays/TekDaysTagLibSpec.groovy. In that one class, we can create as many GSP tags as we want, and they will automatically be available throughout our application. Each tag is a Groovy closure, with optional attrs and body parameters. For example:

```
def backwards = {attrs, body ->
    out << body().reverse()
}
```

This is a custom GSP tag that will reverse whatever text is contained in its body. So, <g:backwards>Hello</g:backwards> will render as olleH. That's not very useful, but it's illustrative nonetheless: That's all there is to it. There are no TLDs (Tag library descriptors) to create, no config files to update, and no supporting classes or interfaces. A TagLib is just a Groovy class, and each tag is a closure with two optional parameters. The first parameter, which we call attrs, is a Map containing any attributes the tag needs. The second, referred to here as body, is a closure. The *names* given to these parameters are not important, but the *order* is; the attributes Map must always be the first parameter. (Notice that our example did not use the attrs parameter, but it still needed to be there so that we could include the body.)

It is so easy to create custom tags in Grails that there is no excuse not to. GSP tags can also be bundled into plugins to make it easier to share them across projects, or to make them available to the public—but that's a topic for another book.[3]

The MessageThread Tag

Our tag will be a bit more complex than the <g:backward> tag, but not all that much more. We are currently using two tags to render our list of messages as links: the <g:each> tag handles the list traversal, and the <g:remoteLink> tag renders the link, with all the Ajax magic hidden inside. Our goal is to replace these with a single tag that will take a list of TekMessage instances, create the same Ajax link for each one, and indent replies to provide the nested view of message threads.

If you haven't already, run the grails create-tag-lib script to create TekDays/grails-app/taglib/com/tekdays/TekDaysTagLib.groovy, and then open that file. It will start looking like this:

forum.2/TekDays/grails-app/taglib/com/tekdays/TekDaysTagLib.groovy
```
package com.tekdays
class TekDaysTagLib {
    static defaultEncodeAs = 'html'
    //static encodeAsForTags = [tagName: 'raw']
}
```

Remove the defaultEncodeAs line—we don't want it here because it would escape all of our tag's output as HTML. Sometimes this can be a good thing, but it's

---

3. *Grails in Action* has an excellent chapter on creating Grails plugins.

not what we're going for right now.[4] Add the following code, and then we'll go over what it's doing:

```groovy
forum.1.2/TekDays/grails-app/taglib/com/tekdays/TekDaysTagLib.groovy
package com.tekdays
class TekDaysTagLib {
    //static encodeAsForTags = [tagName: 'raw']
    def messageThread = {attrs ->
        def messages = attrs.messages.findAll{msg -> !msg.parent}
        processMessages(messages, 0)
    }
    void processMessages(messages, indent){
        messages.each{ msg ->
            def body = "${msg?.author} - ${msg?.subject}"
            out << "<p style='height:35; margin-left:${indent * 20}px;'>"
            out << "${remoteLink(action:'showDetail', id:msg.id,
              update:'details', body)}"
            out << "</p>"
            def children = TekMessage.findAllByParent(msg)
            if (children){
                processMessages(children, indent + 1)
            }
        }
    }
}
```

The first thing we have is our tag closure. It is declared like a controller action, except for the attrs parameter. The tag closure has only two lines because we're moving most of the processing to a method called processMessages().

The tag code's main responsibility is preparing the starting point for the recursive process that is required to get the nesting we are after. To do this, we filter the list that is being passed in the messages attribute, using the findAll method that Groovy adds to Collection. This method will pass each element of a collection to the closure that it takes as a parameter. It will accept or reject the element based on the Boolean result of the closure. We are checking for the existence of a parent property in the TekMessage. The existence of a value evaluates to true in Groovy, so we can shorten a statement like msg.parent == null to !msg.parent. The end result of this line is that we have a collection of *top-level* messages.

The next line passes our filtered collection, along with the number 0, to the processMessages() method. This method takes a collection of messages and an indent value; the first time it's called by the tag, it is given a collection of top-

---

4. encodeAsForTags, which we see commented out by default, works similarly. It allows us to specify a separate encoding for each individual tag.

level messages and the number 0. We use the each() method to iterate over the messages. Instead of using the default it parameter for each(), we are explicitly declaring a msg parameter. msg, then, is a variable that represents each individual message.

Next, we define a body, made up of the message's author and its subject, for our link. Then we begin writing out to the response. The first thing we send to out is a <p> tag, which will help us with positioning our links; notice that we use the indent parameter to determine the amount of margin-left to apply. We next send the <remoteLink> tag to out. There is no multipass resolution of GSPs, so we can't write out other tags from our tag, but we *can* call other tags from our tag and write out the same result that they would have written. That's what we are doing here.

Recall that any GSP tag can be called as a method. The tag name becomes a method name, and the attributes become named parameters. If there is a body, it becomes the last parameter. (Notice that we have action:'showDetail' instead of action="showDetail".) Finally, we close the <p>. As each message in the collection is processed, these lines will be written out, and then we will perform a check to see whether that message has any replies.

We define a children variable, which we load with a call to TekMessage.findAllByParent(). If the message we are working on has any replies, they will be in this collection. We then pass this collection to the processMessages() method recursively, with the indent parameter incremented by 1. This will cause each new level of replies to be indented another 20 pixels and will ensure that all replies are accounted for, no matter how deeply they may be nested.

Having this logic in the page would have been a mess, and it would have been unbearably cumbersome to do this in the controller. A custom tag is the perfect solution to this problem. Indeed, GSP custom tags are the perfect solution to many of the UI problems faced by web developers; that's why they are my second favorite Grails feature (the first favorite is GORM, since I—Dave—am a recovering EJB developer). GSP tags are also a great way to reuse view code and keep your pages DRY.

Not only does this tag prevent us from adding more code to our page, it also allows us to remove some. Let's open TekDays/grails-app/views/tekMessage/ajaxIndex.gsp and replace the five lines encompassing the <g:each> tag with the following single line:

```
forum.1.2/TekDays/grails-app/views/tekMessage/ajaxIndex.gsp
<div id="messageList">
  <g:messageThread messages="${tekMessageInstanceList}" />
</div>
```

In the following figure, we can see what our handiwork looks like. Not bad!

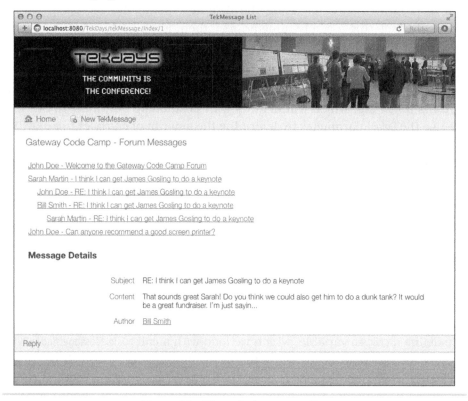

Figure 36—Threaded message list

Summary

Wow! This was a very productive iteration. We implemented one of the most critical features of our application; a community-based event-organizing effort is doomed without good communication. While we were at it, we learned about three important features of Grails. Grails templates are a convenient way of sharing common portions of GSP code and are very helpful when using Ajax. We also learned that Grails makes working with Ajax a snap, while not locking us into any one JavaScript library. Then we got an overview and some good practice with those awesome custom GSP tags.

We'll be moving into security and related issues next, but now it's time for a short break. It's time to catch up on the latest issue of *GroovyMag*[5] to see what's new in this thriving community.

---

5. A monthly e-magazine devoted to all things Groovy: http://groovymag.com.

CHAPTER 8

Knock, Knock: Who's There? Grails Security

Our customer keeps asking us when we are going to add security. We keep telling him, "As soon as we need it." But seriously, as we progress with the TekDays application, it's going to be very helpful to know who's using the application. Not only would that allow us to limit access to certain data or areas of the application, but it would also let us be more intelligent about what we display to our users.

Our goal this time around is to implement a simple security system and see how we can use it to provide a more customized user experience.

Grails Security Options

Grails provides several options when it comes to security, from rolling your own with *controller interceptors* and *filters* to using plugins for the more popular Java security frameworks out there. As of this writing, the main Grails plugin repository has forty-two security-related plugins.

There are plugins for Apache Shiro, CAS, Spring Security, Facebook Connect, and more. There is also the simple yet effective Authentication plugin, which doesn't rely on any external libraries. There are plugins for Captchas, OpenID plugins...you get the picture. For your *next* Grails application, it would be wise to spend some time looking at these plugins to see whether one or more of them might meet your needs.[1] For this project, however, we are going to implement our own solution using Grails filters.

Logging In

Before we get into creating filters and building our security system, let's talk about what we want the system to do. First, we want to know who is currently

---

1. http://grails.org/plugins/

using the system; that is, are they an anonymous user (which is fine), or are they represented by a TekUser instance? Next, we want to restrict access to certain areas of the application based on the current user. For example, only organizers should be able to edit a TekEvent instance, and only organizers *or* volunteers should be able to participate in the event's forum.

For the first step, we will need some sort of login process. We will create two new actions in the TekUserController: login and logout. We will also create a new login view.

Open TekDays/grails-app/controllers/com/tekdays/TekUserController.groovy, and add the following action:

```
def login() {
}
```

Interestingly, we don't need anything in this action; simply having an action with this name will cause the GSP that we are about to create to be rendered. Let's create TekDays/grails-app/views/tekUser/login.gsp and give it the following code:

security.2/TekDays/grails-app/views/tekUser/login.gsp
```
<html>
  <head>
    <meta http-equiv="Content-Type" content="text/html; charset=UTF-8"/>
    <meta name="layout" content="main" />
    <title>Login</title>
  </head>

  <body>
    <g:if test="${flash.message}">
      <div class="message">${flash.message}</div>
    </g:if>

    <g:form action="validate">
      <table>
        <tr class="prop">
          <td class="name">
            <label for="username">User Name:</label>
          </td>

          <td class="value">
            <input type="text" id="username" name="username" value="">
          </td>
        </tr>

        <tr class="prop">
          <td class="name">
            <label for="password">Password:</label>
          </td>
```

```
      <td class="value">
        <input type="password" id="password" name="password" value="">
      </td>
    </tr>

    <tr>
      <td>
      </td>
      <td>
        <input type="submit" value="login"/>
      </td>
    </tr>
  </table>

  </g:form>
 </body>

</html>
```

Simple enough. After a standard Grails message block (which we will need if there are problems during login), we have an HTML form with fields for username and password, followed by a submit button. This page will be merged with our standard header because of this line: <meta name="layout" content="main" />. The final result can be seen in the following figure.

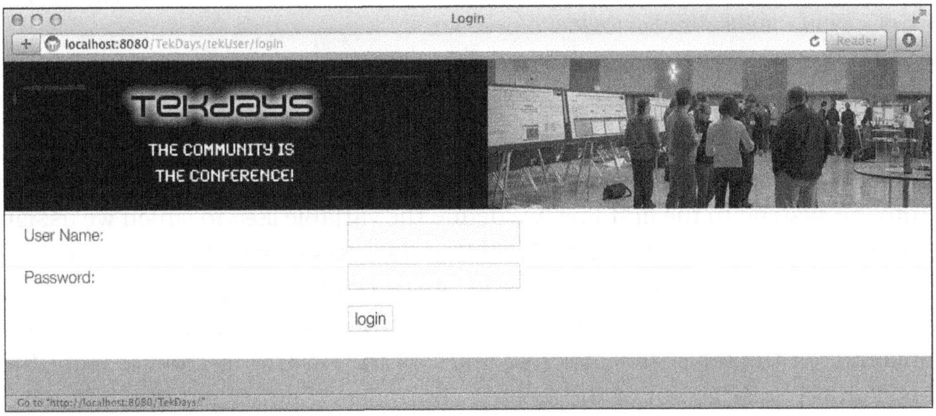

Figure 37—The login page

One important point about this code is the action that we've assigned to the <g:form>: validate. This action will be called when we submit the form. It will reside in the TekUserController and will use the form data to load an existing TekUser if found. We'll create this action now. Open TekDays/grails-app/controllers/com/tekdays/TekUserController.groovy, and add the following action:

```
def validate() {
    def user = TekUser.findByUserName(params.username)
    if (user && user.password == params.password){
        session.user = user
        redirect controller:'tekEvent', action:'index'
    }

    else{
        flash.message = "Invalid username and password."
        render view:'login'
    }
}
```

\\//   **Joe asks:**
ℰ   **We Aren't Going to Use Plain-Text Passwords,**
        Are We?

Don't panic, Joe. This is only a simple example. Before we would put this application in production, we would change this to use encrypted passwords, using something like the DigestUtils class of the Apache Commons project.[a] We might also move the authentication logic to a service class. There are many ways to enhance the security of our application, all of which would fit into the basic structure we are using here.

Our goal for this example is to show the use of Grails filters and to show the structure of a simple authentication system.

---

a.   See http://commons.apache.org/proper/commons-codec/userguide.html.

This action, rather than the login action, does the real work of logging a user into the system. In the first line, we define the variable user, to which we assign the result of a call to TekUser.findByUserName(params.username). Next we check to see whether our user has a value and, if so, whether its password matches params.password. If both of those things are true, then we'll stuff this TekUser instance in the session for later use and call the redirect() method to send the user to the index action of the TekEvent controller. If either is false, we add a message to flash and call the render() method to redisplay the login view.

You'll notice that we used two methods that we didn't define anywhere. The redirect() and render() are added to all controller classes at runtime by Grails. The redirect() method will perform an HTTP redirect. That is, it will return a response to the client that will cause it to make a subsequent call to the URL that is created by the controller and action parameters.

The render() method is very versatile. We used it earlier to respond to an Ajax call. In that instance, we passed it a *template*; here we pass it a *view*. In both cases, the end result was to send a chunk of text back to the client. This method can also be used to render XML, JSON, or any arbitrary text to the client.

In this action, we write to session, which is a Map stored in the *Session* scope. Anything we put there will be available as long as this user is interacting with our application. And since it is a Groovy Map, we can add new key/value pairs by assigning a value to a nonexistent key. There was no user key in session, but we added the key and assigned the value in the following line: session.user = user. We did the same with flash, which is a Map stored in a special scope that lasts for this request and the next, after which the values we put in will be cleared out.

Now that we have a login page and a process for logging a user in, let's see how we can use filters to prompt the user to log in at the appropriate times.

Filters

Filters allow us to hook into, or intercept, the processing of a request. There are interceptors for before, after, and afterView. There are many uses for filters, and you can have as many filters as you need in an application. In our case, we'll use a filter to determine whether a user is logged in when they try to access a "secure" page.

This must be sounding like a broken record (does anyone remember what that is?), but Grails makes implementing filters a snap. Create a Groovy class with a name ending in *Filters*, and place it in the grails-app/conf directory. In this class, define a code block called filters, and then include individual filters as if they were methods. Each filter (method) can take named parameters for controller and action. Calls to this controller and action pair will be intercepted by this filter. (An asterisk can be used as a wildcard to represent any controller or action.) But enough chatter—let's get to the code.

Create a new file called TekDays/grails-app/conf/SecurityFilters.groovy. Open this file, and add the following code:

```
security.2/TekDays/grails-app/conf/SecurityFilters.groovy
class SecurityFilters {
    def filters = {
        doLogin(controller:'*', action:'*'){
            before = {
                if (!controllerName)
                    return true
                def allowedActions = ['show', 'index', 'login',
                                      'validate']
                if (!session.user && !allowedActions.contains(actionName)){
                    redirect(controller:'tekUser', action:'login',
```

```
                            params:['cName': controllerName,
                                    'aName':actionName])
                        return false
                    }
                }
            }
        }
}
```

In our SecurityFilters class, we create a single filter called doLogin with a before interceptor. We use wildcards for both controller and action parameters, which means this filter will be called for all actions. We don't actually want to require the user to log in for every action, so we will fine-tune this filter further.

Every filter has certain properties injected into it by Grails; among these are controllerName and actionName. These represent the original controller and action that the user was trying to access before the filter so rudely interrupted. We will use the actionName to determine whether we really want to filter this call. We'll do this in two steps. In the first step, we'll check to see whether we have a controllerName. If we don't, then we can assume the user is going to the default home page (index.gsp), in which case we will return true. For the second step, we define a List variable with the names of actions that we want to *allow*. Along with the innocuous actions show and index, we included the login and validate actions to avoid unintended login loops. Then in our if comparison, we check to see whether this list contains the current actionName.

The other thing we check in the if comparison is whether we already have a user in the session. If we do not have a user and the current action is not in the allowedActions list, we redirect to the login action of the TekUserController and pass along the controllerName and actionName values in the params parameter. (We'll need them shortly.) In the final line, we return false, which will prevent any other filters (or the original action) from being called.

Now to make this all work nicely, we have to go back and make a few changes to our login view and the two controller actions we added to TekUserController. We want to take advantage of the controllerName and actionName values from the filter. When the filter redirects to the login action, it will pass these values in the params, so we need to do something with them to keep them available. Open TekDays/grails-app/controllers/com/tekdays/TekUserController.groovy, and modify the empty login action like so:

security.2/TekDays/grails-app/controllers/com/tekdays/TekUserController.groovy
```
def login() {
    if (params.cName)
        return [cName:params.cName, aName:params.aName]
}
```

This code checks to see whether those two values are available in params and, if so, passes them on to the view in the returned Map. Next, we'll modify the view to pass these values on to the validate action. Open TekDays/grails-app/views/tekUser/login.gsp, and add the following hidden input elements somewhere inside the <g:form>.

```
security.2/TekDays/grails-app/views/tekUser/login.gsp
<input type="hidden" name="cName" value="${cName}">
<input type="hidden" name="aName" value="${aName}">
```

Now when the form is submitted, the controllerName and actionName values from the filter will be passed on to the validate action. We will now use these values to redirect the user to their original destination on successful login.

Open TekDays/grails-app/controllers/com/tekdays/TekUserController.groovy, and modify the validate action to look like this:

```
security.2/TekDays/grails-app/controllers/com/tekdays/TekUserController.groovy
def validate() {
    def user = TekUser.findByUserName(params.username)

    if (user && user.password == params.password){
        session.user = user

        if (params.cName)
            redirect controller:params.cName, action:params.aName
        else
            redirect controller:'tekEvent', action:'index'
    } else{
        flash.message = "Invalid username and password."
        render view:'login'
    }
}
```

What we're doing here is checking to see whether the controllerName and action-Name (using shortened variables) are available. If they are, we use them to redirect the user; otherwise, we redirect them to the index action of the TekEventController as before. We can come back and change that to the *home* page later (after we add one).

This feature is a bit tricky to show in screenshots, but go ahead and try it. Run the application, and go to the default home page. Choose any of the controller links, and you should come to the list view. Click the "New" button, and you should see the login screen shown in the last figure. Log in using the credentials of one of the users we created earlier, and you should be redirected to the create view that you were aiming at. Good deal!

Logging Out

Since we have a method for logging in and because we like—er, because our customer is quite fond of symmetry, we should add a method for logging out. Don't worry—it'll take only a couple lines of code. Go back to TekDays/grails-app/controllers/com/tekdays/TekUserController, and add a logout action, like so:

security.2/TekDays/grails-app/controllers/com/tekdays/TekUserController.groovy
```groovy
def logout = {
    session.user = null
    redirect(uri:'/')
}
```

Since the way that our filter determines whether a user is logged in is by the existence of a value in the user key, we set that key to null to "log them out." We don't need to check for a user key before we do this; if it doesn't exist, it will be created and set to null. Then, to send the logged-out user back to the home page, we use the redirect() method. In most cases, this method will take an action, or a controller and action pair. But it can also take a url, or, as in this case, a uri. Simply redirecting to a URI of / will return us to the home page no matter where we are in the application. Pretty handy!

Now we can log in and out of the system, but the only way we can do either directly is to type the appropriate URL into our browser (for example, http://localhost:8080/TekDays/tekUser/login). That's not very Web 2.0. It's more like Web 0.5. What would be great is if we had a login/logout *toggle* that we could display where appropriate. Sounds like a great place for a custom tag!

Go back to our taglib at TekDays/grails-app/taglib/com/tekdays/TekDaysTagLib.groovy and add a new tag closure called loginToggle:

security.2/TekDays/grails-app/taglib/com/tekdays/TekDaysTagLib.groovy
```groovy
def loginToggle = {
    out << "<div style='margin: 15px 0 40px;'>"
    if (request.getSession(false) && session.user){
        out << "<span style='float:left; margin-left: 15px'>"
        out << "Welcome ${session.user}."
        out << "</span><span style='float:right;margin-right:15px'>"
        out << "<a href='${createLink(controller:'tekUser', action:'logout')}'>"
        out << "Logout </a></span>"
    } else{
        out << "<span style='float:right;margin-right:10px'>"
        out << "<a href='${createLink(controller:'tekUser', action:'login')}'>"
        out << "Login </a></span>"
    }
    out << "</div><br/>"
}
```

This tag doesn't need any attributes or a body, so we skip the closure parameters altogether. We start by writing out an opening <div>. Then we check to see whether a user exists. If we have a user, we output a "Welcome" message and a link to allow them to log out. For the message, we use ${session.user} inside a GString. (This will lead to a call to the TekUser.toString() method, which we defined earlier.) For the link, we use a regular anchor tag along with the <createLink> tag, called as a method. If there is no user, we just output a link to allow the user to log in. There's also a little CSS, but that's not too exciting.

We'll use this new tag in TekDays/grails-app/views/layouts/main.gsp, so go ahead and open that file. Add the <g:loginToggle> tag, as shown here:

```
security.2/TekDays/grails-app/views/layouts/main.gsp
<div id="logo" role="banner">
  <a href="${createLink(uri: '/')}">
  <img src="${resource(dir: 'images', file: 'td_logo.png')}"
  alt="TekDays"/></a>
  <g:loginToggle />
</div>
```

We can see how our new custom tag looks in the following figure. Much better.

Figure 38—The loginToggle tag in action

Summary

That went quickly! It's OK—you can use the extra time to do a little experimenting. Maybe you can try using filters to add logging or something exciting like that. We now have the beginnings of a workable security system in place for TekDays. It's not as robust as those provided by the Spring Security or Shiro plugins, but it'll work for our purposes. We also have a new custom tag in our growing tag library.

Next up, we'll start tying some of these pieces together with a more useful home page and a dashboard view for event organizers. We'll see how Grails allows us to build much more than single-domain views and that MVC doesn't have to be a collection of silos. It just keeps getting better!

CHAPTER 9

Big-Picture Views

So far, the views we've been building have been focused on a single domain class. The Grails convention-based MVC architecture allows us to build these types of views quickly, and they play an important role in most applications. But most applications—TekDays included—will also need a way to interact with data from multiple domain classes at a time.

The person taking on the responsibility of organizing a community technical event has a big job on their hands; it's an exciting and rewarding job, but a big one nonetheless. We're here to help that hard-working, visionary individual, and one way we can do that is to provide a more convenient way for them to see details about their event and to perform common tasks. In this iteration, we're going to implement an organizer's dashboard view. This view will not be tied to any one domain class but will interact with most (if not all) of them at one time. We might even hit data that is not from our domain.

Before we launch into what will arguably be the most complex view of our application, let's warm up with another view that needs some work. Our home page could really use some love. The list of controller links is getting kind of old, so let's warm up our GSP muscles with a home page makeover.

Home Page Makeover

The application home page can be found in the root view directory: TekDays/grails-app/views/index.gsp.

Let's open this file now to see what we have to work with:

security.2/TekDays/grails-app/views/index.gsp

```
<!DOCTYPE html>
<html>
  <head>
    <meta name="layout" content="main"/>
    <title>Welcome to Grails</title>
```

```
    <!-- embedded CSS omitted for the sake of space -->
  </head>
  <body>
    <a href="#page-body" class="skip"><g:message
      code="default.link.skip.label" default="Skip to content&hellip;"/></a>
    <div id="status" role="complementary">
      <h1>Application Status</h1>
      <ul>
        <li>App version: <g:meta name="app.version"/></li>
        <li>Grails version: <g:meta name="app.grails.version"/></li>
        <li>Groovy version: ${GroovySystem.getVersion()}</li>
        <li>JVM version: ${System.getProperty('java.version')}</li>
        <li>Reloading active: ${grails.util.Environment.reloadingAgentEnabled}</li>
        <li>Controllers: ${grailsApplication.controllerClasses.size()}</li>
        <li>Domains: ${grailsApplication.domainClasses.size()}</li>
        <li>Services: ${grailsApplication.serviceClasses.size()}</li>
        <li>Tag Libraries: ${grailsApplication.tagLibClasses.size()}</li>
      </ul>
      <h1>Installed Plugins</h1>
      <ul>
        <g:each var="plugin"
          in="${applicationContext.getBean('pluginManager').allPlugins}">
          <li>${plugin.name} - ${plugin.version}</li>
        </g:each>
      </ul>
    </div>
    <div id="page-body" role="main">
      <h1>Welcome to Grails</h1>
      <p>Congratulations, you have successfully started your first Grails
        application! At the moment this is the default page, feel free to
        modify it to either redirect to a controller or display whatever
        content you may choose. Below is a list of controllers that are
        currently deployed in this application, click on each to execute
        its default action:</p>

      <div id="controller-list" role="navigation">
        <h2>Available Controllers:</h2>
        <ul>
          <g:each var="c"
            in="${grailsApplication.controllerClasses.sort { it.fullName } }">
            <li class="controller"><g:link
              controller="${c.logicalPropertyName}">${c.fullName}</g:link>
            </li>
          </g:each>
        </ul>
      </div>
    </div>
  </body>
</html>
```

We'll be getting rid of most of this, but it is interesting to see what's going on here. For example, there is a <g:each> tag that is iterating over a list of all the controllers in the application and creating a link for each one. Looking at things like grailsApplication.controllerClasses gives you an idea of the types of things you can do with Grails as you move on from here. Grails is by no means a shallow framework!

As interesting as that code is, it doesn't do what we need right now, so we'll get rid of everything in the <body> section. In the <head>, we'll remove the <style> block of page-specific CSS and change the <title> to the name and slogan of our application. We'll replace the <body> with a welcome paragraph and a few <div> blocks to represent the major tasks in TekDays. The end result should look like this:

bigger.2/TekDays/grails-app/views/index.gsp

```
<!DOCTYPE html>
<html>
  <head>
    <meta name="layout" content="main"/>
    <title>TekDays - The Community is the Conference!</title>
  </head>
  <body>
    <div id="welcome">
      <br />
      <h3>Welcome to TekDays.com</h3>
      <p>TekDays.com is a site dedicated to assisting individuals and
         communities to organize technology conferences.  To bring great
         minds with common interests and passions together for the good
         of greater geekdom!</p>
    </div>
    <div class="homeCell">
      <h3>Find a Tek Event</h3>
      <p> See if there's a technical event in the works that strikes your
         fancy. If there is, you can volunteer to help or just let the
         organizers know that you'd be interested in attending.
         Everybody has a role to play.</p>
      <span class="buttons" >
        <g:link controller="tekEvent" action="index">Find a Tek Event</g:link>
      </span>
    </div>
    <div class="homeCell">
      <h3>Organize a Tek Event</h3>
      <p>If you don't see anything that suits your interest and location,
         then why not get the ball rolling.  It's easy to get started and
         there may be others out there ready to get behind you to make it
         happen.</p>
      <span class="buttons" >
        <g:link controller="tekEvent" action="create"> Organize a Tek Event</g:link>
```

```
      </span>
    </div>
    <div class="homeCell">
      <h3>Sponsor a Tek Event</h3>
      <p>If you are part of a business or organization that is involved in
          technology then sponsoring a tek event would be a great way to
          let the community know that you're there and you're involved.</p>
      <span class="buttons" >
        <g:link controller="sponsor" action="create">Sponsor a Tek Event</g:link>
      </span>
    </div>
  </body>
</html>
```

That's kind of a long listing, but it's not very complicated. We broke the page up into four blocks: an introduction and one section each for the three main activities users will do in our application. There are other activities, but they will be branches off of these three—browsing events, creating an event, or becoming a sponsor. In the following figure, we can see our new home page in all of its glory (so to speak).

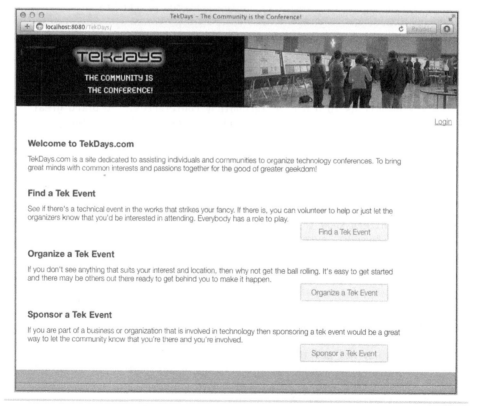

Figure 39—The TekDays home page

Creating a New Controller

Now that we're all warmed up and ready, we'll get to work on the new organizer's dashboard view. To keep our overall architecture clean and not confuse the conventions that have proved so helpful to us, we will create a new controller for the dashboard view and any related views. We'll use the create-controller script to do this:

```
$ grails create-controller com.tekdays.Dashboard
```

The script creates the file TekDays/grails-app/controllers/com/tekdays/DashboardController.groovy, along with the corresponding test file TekDays/test/unit/com/tekdays/DashboardControllerSpec.groovy. It also creates the TekDays/grails-app/views/dashboard directory, where our new controller will look for views.

Controllers and Conventions

The Grails convention of naming a controller with a domain class name followed by *Controller*, and the way that the generate-all script takes a domain class and generates a conventionally named controller and standard views in a directory with the same name, can make it seem like everything must be based on a domain class. The fact is that aside from the work of generate-all, there is no link between a domain class and a controller.

Any domain class can be accessed from any controller. The static methods that Grails adds to domain classes (get(), list(), and so on) are available in any controller.

The real convention-based link is between controllers and *views*. An action in a controller will, unless directed otherwise, attempt to render a view named after the action, in a directory named after the controller. For example, a bar action in FooController will attempt to render the view in ../grails-app/views/foo/bar.gsp.

This controller will be responsible for rendering the dashboard view and supplying it with the necessary data. To be clearer about what data we need, we'll work on the view first. Once we have that done, we'll come back to the DashboardController.

Designing the Dashboard View

The purpose of the dashboard view is to give event organizers and volunteers an "at-a-glance" view of the most pertinent information regarding their event, with links to get to where they need to go. This will be their starting place when they come to work on their event.

We'll discuss the design more as we go along, but to get started, create an empty file called TekDays/grails-app/views/dashboard/dashboard.gsp, and add the following code:

```
bigger.2/TekDays/grails-app/views/dashboard/dashboard.gsp
<html>
  <head>
    <title>TekDays - Dashboard</title>
    <meta name="layout" content="main" />
  </head>
  <body>
  </body>
</html>
```

This page will have a good amount of content in it, so in order to keep it manageable from a coding standpoint, we'll compose the page out of a series of templates. Our main dashboard page will consist of several <g:render> tags, which can easily be rearranged and styled as necessary. We'll add these tags now and then create the templates they refer to. In dashboard.gsp, add the following code between the opening and closing <body> tags:

```
bigger.2/TekDays/grails-app/views/dashboard/dashboard.gsp
<div id="event" style='margin:10px 10px 10px 10px'>
  <g:render template="event" model="${['event':event]}" />
</div>
<div id="tasks" style='margin:10px 10px 10px 10px'>
  <g:render template="tasks" model="${['tasks':tasks]}" />
</div>
<div id="volunteers" style='margin:10px 10px 10px 10px'>
  <g:render template="volunteers" model="${['volunteers':volunteers]}" />
</div>
<div id="messages" style='margin:10px 10px 10px 10px'>
  <g:render template="messages" model="${[messages:messages]}" />
</div>
<div id="sponsors" style='margin:10px 10px 10px 10px'>
  <g:render template="sponsors" model="${[sponsorships:sponsorships]}" />
</div>
```

We added several <div> tags containing <g:render> tags. We can tweak the styling on these elements or change their order or what have you. Now we can address each template on its own, which will help our discussion (as well as our code) to be more organized. Recall that the <g:render> tag will insert the final HTML of the designated template inside the containing element—in this case, the <div>. Let's start with the template for the basic event information.

Basic Event Information

In this first template we'll have information from the TekEvent itself, such as name, city, dates, and venue. We'll display the event name and city at the top center and then build a simple table to display the other data elements. Create the file TekDays/grails-app/views/dashboard/_event.gsp, and give it the following code:

```
bigger.2/TekDays/grails-app/views/dashboard/_event.gsp
<span style="text-align:center">
  <h1>${event}</h1>
</span>
<table>
  <tr>
    <td>
      Start Date: <g:formatDate format="MMM/dd/yyyy" date="${event.startDate}"/>
    </td>

    <td>
      <g:if test="${event.endDate}">
        End Date: <g:formatDate format="MMM/dd/yyyy" date="${event.endDate}"/>
      </g:if>
    </td>
  </tr>

  <tr>
    <td>
      Venue: ${event.venue}
    </td>

    <td>
      Number of potential attendees: ${event.respondents.size()}
    </td>
  </tr>
</table>
```

Notice that we also displayed the number of potential attendees. This is not a data element itself, but is the count of the respondents collection property. This is the type of information that we will want at a glance; the complete list of respondents' email addresses would be overkill here.

Tasks

Next up is the task list. This will be an abbreviated list of the first few incomplete tasks, with a link to go to the full task list.

Create TekDays/grails-app/views/dashboard/_tasks.gsp, and add this code:

bigger.2/TekDays/grails-app/views/dashboard/_tasks.gsp
```
<h3>Things to do</h3>
<table>
  <thead>
    <tr>
      <th>Task Title</th>
      <th>Due Date</th>
      <th>Assigned To</th>
    </tr>
  </thead>
  <g:each in="${tasks}" var="task">
    <tr>
      <td>${task.title}</td>
      <td>
        <g:formatDate format="MM/dd/yyyy" date="${task.dueDate}" />
      </td>
      <td>
        ${task.assignedTo}
      </td>
    </tr>
  </g:each>
</table>
<g:link controller="task" action="index" id="${event.id}">
  View all ${event.tasks.size()} tasks for this event.
</g:link>
```

The template starts out with a heading, followed by a table with three columns displaying the title, dueDate, and assignedTo properties of each Task. Then we finish off with a link to the rest of the tasks for this event. (Notice that we take advantage of the GSP being one big GString by embedding a Groovy expression in the middle of the <g:link> body.)

Volunteers

For the volunteers template, create TekDays/grails-app/views/dashboard/_volunteers.gsp, and enter the following code:

bigger.2/TekDays/grails-app/views/dashboard/_volunteers.gsp
```
<h3>Volunteers</h3>

<table>
  <thead>
    <tr>
      <th>Name</th>
      <th>Email Address</th>
      <th>Web Site</th>
    </tr>
  </thead>
```

```
<g:each in="${volunteers}" var="volunteer">
  <tr>
    <td>
      <g:link controller="tekUser" action="show" id="${volunteer.id}">
        ${volunteer.fullName}
      </g:link>
    </td>
    <td>
      <a href="mailto:${volunteer.email}">
        ${volunteer.email}
      </a>
    </td>
    <td>
      <a href="http://${volunteer.website}">
        ${volunteer.website}
      </a>
    </td>
  </tr>
</g:each>
</table>
```

The volunteers template starts out the same as the tasks template with a header, a table with three columns, and a row for each volunteer. One difference is that we are not limiting the list of volunteers; the whole gang will be there. Some other differences are the links that we are building in. Notice the <g:link> tag that we use inside the fullName <td>. This will create a link to the show action of the TekUser controller with the id of the given volunteer. We also used HTML anchor tags to turn the volunteer's email and website into links. Now the organizer has a quick way to fire off an email to a volunteer.

Messages

Next, we'll have a top-level list of the messages in the forum. Create a blank file called TekDays/grails-app/views/dashboard/_messages.gsp, and code it as follows:

bigger.2/TekDays/grails-app/views/dashboard/_messages.gsp
```
<h3>Forum Messages</h3>
<table>
  <thead>
    <tr>
      <th>Author</th>
      <th>Subject</th>
      <th>Content</th>
    </tr>
  </thead>
  <g:each in="${messages}" var="msg">
    <tr>
      <td>
```

```
      <g:link controller="tekUser" action="show" id="${msg.author.id}">
        ${msg.author}
      </g:link>
    </td>
    <td>
      ${msg.subject}
    </td>
    <td>
      ${msg.content[0..Math.min(msg.content.size() -1, 24)]}
      ${msg.content.size() > 25 ? '...' : ''}
    </td>
  </tr>
  </g:each>
</table>
<g:link controller="tekMessage" action="index" id="${event.id}">
  View threaded messages for this event.
</g:link>
```

This code is similar to the others: a table with three columns and a <g:each> tag to iterate over the messages and fill the table. The messages list will contain only top-level messages (no replies), but this will be handled in the controller. One interesting thing that we did in this template is truncate the content if it is more than 25 characters long.

Groovy allows us to retrieve a portion of a String using a *range*, as in the following example:

bigger.2/TekDays/scripts/substring_example.groovy
```
def s = 'Grails is fun!'
assert s[0..5] == 'Grails'
```

In our template, this line:

```
${msg.content[0..Math.min(msg.content.size() -1, 24)]}
```

uses a *range* to get the first 25 characters of the content property of the message. To avoid getting an IndexOutOfBounds exception if the content is shorter than 25 characters, we used Math.min(). In the next line:

```
${msg.content.size() > 25 ? '...' : ''}
```

we tacked on an ellipsis, using a Java *ternary* operator. If we were going to do this anywhere else, it would be another good candidate for a custom tag.

Sponsors

This last template will contain a Sponsor list. But as we discussed in *Many-to-Many Relationships*, on page 49, the TekEvent has no direct relationship with the Sponsor class; we have to work with the intermediate class Sponsorship. (Our template will actually contain information from both Sponsor and Sponsorship.) Create a blank file called TekDays/grails-app/views/dashboard/_sponsors.gsp, and add the following code:

```
bigger.2/TekDays/grails-app/views/dashboard/_sponsors.gsp
<h3>Sponsors</h3>
<table>
  <thead>
    <tr>
      <th>Name</th>
      <th>Web Site</th>
      <th>Contribution</th>
    </tr>
  </thead>

  <g:each in="${sponsorships}" var="s">
    <tr>
      <td>
        <g:link controller="sponsor" action="show" id="${s.sponsor.id}">
          ${s.sponsor.name}
        </g:link>
      </td>

      <td>
        <a href="${s.sponsor.website}">
          ${s.sponsor.website}
        </a>
      </td>
      <td>
        ${s.contributionType}
      </td>
    </tr>
  </g:each>
</table>
```

The <g:each> tag in this template is iterating over a list of Sponsorship instances. Each instance is being stored in the variable s. To get the sponsor.name and sponsor.website properties, we accessed the sponsor property of the Sponsorship class like this: ${s.sponsor.name}. The contributionType is a property of the Sponsor~ class, so we can access it directly. We also implemented links to ' show view and the sponsor's website, the same way we did for ' template.

Now we have the basic components of our dashboard page. W to it later and add some features to make it more useful, b close the feedback loop and see this view in action. To add the controller action that will collect the data we r view.

Adding the Dashboard Action

We can tell from looking at the code for our dashboard view that it will need the following data elements when it is rendered: event, tasks, volunteers, messages, and sponsorships. The first of these is a single TekEvent instance; the rest are collections of related objects.

Some of these collections need to be filtered or limited in some way. This will also be done in the controller action.

Let's see how easy this can be. Open TekDays/grails-app/controllers/com/tekdays/Dashboard-Controller.groovy. The empty index action should already be there. Right after that, add the dashboard action:

```
bigger.2/TekDays/grails-app/controllers/com/tekdays/DashboardController.groovy
package com.tekdays
class DashboardController {

    def index() { }

    def dashboard = {
        def event = TekEvent.get(params.id)
        if (event){
            if(event.organizer.userName == session.user.userName ||
                event.volunteers.collect{it.userName}.contains(
                                                    session.user.userName)){
                def tasks = Task.findAllByEventAndCompleted(event, false,
                                    max:3, sort:'dueDate', order: 'asc'])
                def volunteers = event.volunteers
                def messages = TekMessage.findAllByEventAndParentIsNull(event,
                                            [sort:'id', order:'desc'])
                def sponsorships = event.sponsorships
                return [event:event, tasks:tasks, volunteers:volunteers,
                        messages:messages, sponsorships:sponsorships]
            }
            else{
              flash.message = "Access to dashboard for ${event.name} denied."
              redirect controller:'tekEvent', action:'index'
            }
        }
        else{
            flash.message = "No event was found with an id of ${params.id}"
            redirect controller:'tekEvent', action:'index'
        }
    }
}
```

This action expects an id in the params Map. We first use that value to retrieve ⟨ev⟩ent instance, using the TekEvent.get() method. The rest of the code is wrapped in a couple of if blocks. If the event is null, we add a message to flash and redirect the user to the TekEvent list. If the event is not null, then we check to see whether the logged-in user has access to this view.

This view is for event organizers or volunteers, so we check to see whether the logged-in user (session.user) is either the organizer or a user in the list of volunteers. Determining whether the logged-in user is the organizer is a simple comparison, but determining whether the logged-in user is among the volunteers is a bit tricky. We use the collect() method on event.volunteers to iterate over the Set and return a list containing the userName of each volunteer. Then we call the contains() method on that list, passing in the userName of the logged-in user. If that test is passed, we begin retrieving the rest of the data.

The tasks variable is a list of Task instances associated with this TekEvent. We could use the tasks property of the TekEvent class, as we will do with others, but we want to limit the list to the first three incomplete tasks. Dynamic finders give us an easy way to do this. All of Grails' dynamic finders allow a Map parameter, which can contain the following elements: offset, max, sort, and order. These values are used for pagination and sorting (which we get in the scaffolded list views, for example). We take advantage of max to limit our list to three items and use sort to get the tasks that are most urgent.

We don't need to do anything special with the volunteers list, so we just take the event.volunteers property. The messages list should show the most recent messages, so we use a dynamic finder again (this time using the IsNull comparator) and pass in parameters in the Map to do a descending sort on the id property.

The sponsorships list is also a simple one, so we just use the sponsorships property of the TekEvent. Once we've defined and loaded all of the data elements our dashboard view needs, we return them in the params Map.

Now, if we log in as the event organizer or a volunteer and navigate to http://localhost:8080/TekDays/dashboard/dashboard/1, we're greeted with the page shown in Figure 40, *TekDays organizer's dashboard*, on page 144.

Adding a Menu

Our dashboard view gives event organizers and volunteers a good look at most aspects of their event, but it would be nice if they could take some actions from there, too. We'll add a menu to the dashboard to enable that.

Open TekDays/grails-app/views/dashboard/dashboard.gsp, and add the following code to the top of the <body> section:

Figure 40—TekDays organizer's dashboard

bigger.2/TekDays/grails-app/views/dashboard/dashboard.gsp

```
<div class="nav" role="navigation">
  <ul>
    <li><a class="home" href="${createLink(uri: '/')}">Home</a></li>
    <li><g:link class="create" controller="task" action="create"> Create
```

```
      Task</g:link></li>
    <li><g:link class="create" controller="sponsorship" action="create">Add
      Sponsor</g:link></li>
    <li><g:link class="list" controller="sponsor" action="index"> All
      Sponsors</g:link></li>
  </ul>
</div>
```

This code is mostly borrowed from the scaffolded pages that Grails gave us. We kept the "Home" menu item and added items to create new tasks and sponsorships. We also added a menu item to list all sponsors. (This might be useful to see who else is interested in sponsoring technical events.) We are using the <g:link> and <g:createLink> tags, which we discussed earlier. One interesting thing here is the CSS classes that we are using: home, create, and list. These classes are provided by Grails and can be found in TekDays/web-app/css/main.css.

In the following figure, we can see what our dashboard menu looks like.

Figure 41—The dashboard menu

Linking to the Dashboard

Now that we have a dashboard view, we need to provide an easy way to get to it. The TekEvent show view is a logical place to provide a link to the dashboard. Open TekDays/grails-app/views/tekEvent/show.gsp, and add the highlighted code to the "nav" <div> near the top of the file.

```
bigger.2/TekDays/grails-app/views/tekEvent/show.gsp
<div class="nav" role="navigation">
  <ul>
    <li><a class="home" href="${createLink(uri: '/')}"><g:message
      code="default.home.label"/></a></li>
    <li><g:link class="list" action="index"><g:message
      code="default.list.label" args="[entityName]" /></g:link></li>
```

```
    <li><g:link class="create" action="create"><g:message
      code="default.new.label" args="[entityName]" /></g:link></li>
➤   <li><g:link class="list" controller="dashboard" action="dashboard"
➤     id="${tekEventInstance.id}"> Event Dashboard</g:link></li>
  </ul>
</div>
```

Again, we just copied the existing menu code and modified the <g:link> tag to go to the dashboard action of the DashboardController. Notice that the variable used to represent the TekEvent instance is tekEventInstance, instead of event as we have been using. When modifying an existing view, we have to use the variable names that are passed to it by the controller. (To find out what they are, we can just look at the controller action.)

The updated menu on the show view is shown in the following figure.

Figure 42—The event show view menu

Summary

We now have a convenient dashboard view to help event organizers and volunteers keep an eye on their event, and we have an easy way for them to get to it. We have security in place so that only authorized users can get to the dashboard. As a bonus, we have a much friendlier and more helpful home page. And while we got all that done, we learned how to create a controller that is not tied to a domain class and use it to populate and access views that span multiple domain classes. We also got some good practice working with GSP views and templates. (Our customer is impressed, too, and that's always a good thing.)

In the next iteration, we'll be looking for a good way to add search capabilities to TekDays. This will introduce us to more of the coolness that is GORM and to the Grails plugin architecture.

CHAPTER 10

Seek, and You Shall Find

Any nontrivial application needs to have some sort of search mechanism. TekDays is no exception. In fact, our customer informed us of three different places where he wants us to incorporate some sort of search behavior. Well, actually he wanted more than that, but we had to take a stand against scope creep. For now, we will implement these three: first, when a user logs into TekDays, we will find any TekEvent that has them as the organizer; second, we will also find any TekEvent for which they are a volunteer (both of these will show up on the home page); and finally, we will have the traditional search feature where users can look for a TekEvent based on the properties of the event. As we implement these new features, we will describe three common ways of searching and finding objects with Grails.

Search Using Dynamic Finders

When an event organizer logs into TekDays, we should give them a direct link to the event, or events, that they are organizing. These folks are busy; we don't want to waste their time. Fortunately, this is very easy to do using Grails' dynamic finders (introduced in *Introducing GORM*, on page 41).

Here's the plan. When the user logs in, we will find all the TekEvent instances that have this user assigned to the organizer property. We will then display links to the show view for each TekEvent on the home page.

The search part of this feature is pretty simple, but we have to decide just where to do it and how to display it. Let's have a brief design session to see what we can come up with. We want to show the organizer's events on the home page, but the home page, unlike most pages in a Grails application, is not rendered from a controller action. That means that we can't pass the event list to it in a model (a Map). We could retrieve the list right from the page with code like this:

```
<g:each in="${TekEvent.findAllByOrganizer(session.user)}" var="event">
  <!-- code to display event here -->
</g:each>
```

There are a couple of problems with this approach. First, we are putting more code in our page than we should. Second, we would want to do this only if we have a logged-in user, so we would have to wrap this code in something like this:

```
<g:if test="${session.user}">
  <!-- each loop and corresponding code goes here -->
</g:if>
```

This would work, but it's ugly. So, what would be a good way to load and display these events every time the page loads for a logged-in event organizer? If you said "custom tag," you get a gold star by your name. This is an excellent case for a custom tag. Let's open our tag library, TekDays/grails-app/taglib/com/tek-days/TekDaysTagLib.groovy, and add the following code at the end of the class:

```
seek.2/TekDays/grails-app/taglib/com/tekdays/TekDaysTagLib.groovy
def organizerEvents = {
    if (request.getSession(false) && session.user){
        def events = TekEvent.findAllByOrganizer(session.user)
        if (events){
            out << "<div style='margin-left:25px; margin-top:25px; width:85%'>"
            out << "<h3>Events you are organizing:</h3>"
            out << "<ol>"
            events.each{
                out << "<li><a href='"
                out << "${createLink(controller:'tekEvent',action:'show',
                        id:it.id)}'>"
                out << "${it}</a></li>"
            }
            out << "</ol>"
            out << "</div>"
        }
    }
}
```

We defined a closure called organizerEvents that creates a tag called <g:organiz-erEvents>. This closure takes no parameters, which means that our new tag will not have a body or any attributes. Inside the closure, the first thing we do is check to see whether there is a logged-in user. (Recall from Chapter 8, *Knock, Knock: Who's There? Grails Security*, on page 121, that we store the logged-in user in session.user.)

If we have a user, we use the dynamic finder TekEvent.findAllByOrganizer() to get a list of TekEvent instances. In the next line, we check to see whether that call returned anything. In Groovy, a collection reference evaluates to false if it is null or empty. The next few lines set up a <div> and an <ol>.

Next, we use the each() method to iterate over our list of events and create a <li> and an <a> for each event. Notice how we use ${it} for the body of the <a> tag; this will call the toString() on the TekEvent, which returns name and city properties. Finally, we close out the ordered list and the <div>.

Now we can retrieve the list of events and display them on our home page by adding a single line of code. In TekDays/grails-app/views/index.gsp, add the following highlighted line:

seek.2/TekDays/grails-app/views/index.gsp
```
  <h3>Welcome to TekDays.com</h3>
  <p>TekDays.com is a site dedicated to assisting individuals and
     communities to organize technology conferences.  To bring great
     minds with common interests and passions together for the good
     of greater geekdom!</p>
</div>

<g:organizerEvents />
<div class="homeCell">
  <h3>Find a Tek Event</h3>

  <p> See if there's a technical event in the works that strikes your fancy.
     If there is, you can volunteer to help or just let the
     organizers know that you'd be interested in attending.
     Everybody has a role to play.</p>

  <span class="buttons" >
    <g:link controller="tekEvent" action="index">Find a Tek Event</g:link>
  </span>
</div>
```

Not only have we avoided putting a bunch of business logic in our page, but we also have a tag that can easily be reused in other pages as needed. We don't know about you, but we'll sure sleep better at night.

Now that we have this nifty feature, let's make one more change to make it easier to see it in action. Currently, the validate action of the TekUserController redirects users to the TekEventController.index action after a successful login. We want to change that to redirect to the home page. Open TekDays/grails-app/controllers/com/tekdays/TekUserController.groovy, and find the line in the validate action that looks like this:

```
redirect(controller:'tekEvent', action:'index')
```

Change that to look like the following highlighted line:

seek.2/TekDays/grails-app/controllers/com/tekdays/TekUserController.groovy

```groovy
def validate() {
    def user = TekUser.findByUserName(params.username)
    if (user && user.password == params.password){
        session.user = user
        if (params.cName)
            redirect controller:params.cName, action:params.aName
        else
            redirect(uri:'/')
    }
    else{
        flash.message = "Invalid username and password."
        render view:'login'
    }
}
```

In the following figure, we can see what this looks like after our friend John Doe started up a couple more events.

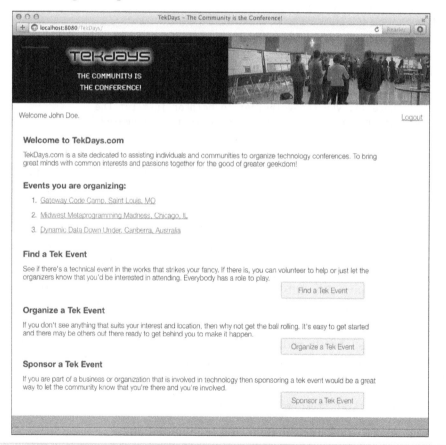

Figure 43—TekDays home page with organizer events

Hibernate Criteria Builder

Dynamic finders are great, and as you work with Grails, you will find yourself using them again and again, but they can take you only so far. For one thing, they are limited to top-level properties of the class—you cannot use dynamic finders to search relationships.

Our next search feature is to find TekEvent instances for which a logged-in user has volunteered. Volunteers for an event are in the volunteers collection, which is the result of a one-to-many relationship between TekEvent and TekUser. To search relationships, we must turn to a different tool in the Grails toolbox.

The Criteria Builder in Grails is a very powerful and flexible tool for retrieving objects. It is based on the Hibernate Criteria API, so you can dig deeper by studying that technology.[1] However, this *is* Grails we're talking about, so you can do plenty with this tool by following some simple examples.

All Grails domain classes have a static createCriteria() method that returns a HibernateCriteriaBuilder instance. This builder has a list() method that takes a closure. Inside this closure, we can define the criteria for our search.

Here's an example:

```
def g3Events = TekEvent.createCriteria().list{
  and{
    gt('startDate', new Date())
    or{
      ilike('description', '%groovy%')
      ilike('description', '%grails%')
      ilike('description', '%griffon%')
    }
  }
}
```

This code produces a list of the technical events that you would be likely to find us attending. More specifically, the g3Events list would contain any TekEvent that contained the words *Groovy*, *Grails*, or *Griffon* in the description property and whose startDate is still in the future. Notice how we have an or block nested inside an and block. This type of nesting of logical blocks can be much clearer and easier to read than an equivalent SQL statement.

Another nice feature of Criteria Builders is that relationship properties can easily be searched. This is also done with nested criteria blocks. Let's see how this looks:

---

1. http://docs.jboss.org/hibernate/orm/3.3/reference/en-US/html/querycriteria.html

```
def contegixEvents = TekEvent.createCriteria().list{
  sponsorships{
    sponsor{
      eq('name', 'Contegix')
    }
  }
}
```

This code loads contegixEvents with all TekEvent instances that Contegix is sponsoring. It does this by searching the sponsorships property, which is a collection of Sponsorship instances. That is represented by the first block. A Sponsorship has a sponsor property that is of type Sponsor. That's the second block. Then, within the sponsor block, we check for a name property that is equal to Contegix.

This last technique is the one we will use to find all events that a logged-in user has volunteered for. Since we want to display this list on the home page as we did for the organizer's event list, we will once again take advantage of Grails' custom tags. Let's open TekDays/grails-app/taglib/com/tekdays/TekDaysTagLib.groovy and add the following tag code:

```
seek.2/TekDays/grails-app/taglib/com/tekdays/TekDaysTagLib.groovy
def volunteerEvents = {
    if (request.getSession(false) && session.user){
        def events = TekEvent.createCriteria().list{
            volunteers{
                eq('id', session.user?.id)
            }
        }
        if (events){
            out << "<div style='margin-left:25px; margin-top:25px; width:85%'>"
            out << "<h3>Events you volunteered for:</h3>"
            out << "<ul>"
            events.each{
                out << "<li><a href='"
                out << "${createLink(controller:'tekEvent',action:'show',
                        id:it.id)}'>"
                out << "${it}</a></li>"
            }
            out << "</ul>"
            out << "</div>"
        }
    }
}
```

Much of the code for our <g:volunteerEvents> tag is the same as the code for the <g:organizerEvents> tag we created earlier. Let's take a look at the bits that are different. The most important difference is that we are using a Criteria Builder to load the events list. We are searching the volunteers collection for a TekUser with an id that is equal to the id of the logged-in user (session.user). The next difference is the heading, which isn't all that interesting. And finally, in this tag we are accessing the id of the session.user instead of the user by itself.

To put this new tag to use, open TekDays/grails-app/views/index.gsp, and add the highlighted line:

```
seek.1.2/TekDays/grails-app/views/index.gsp
  <h3>Welcome to TekDays.com</h3>
  <p>TekDays.com is a site dedicated to assisting individuals and
      communities to organize technology conferences.  To bring great
      minds with common interests and passions together for the good
      of greater geekdom!</p>
</div>
<g:organizerEvents />
<g:volunteerEvents />
```

Now when a user who has volunteered to help out with one or more events logs in, the home page will look similar to Figure 44, *TekDays home page with volunteer events*, on page 154.

The Big Guns: The Searchable Plugin

So far, in this iteration we have implemented internal searches to add features for our users—and right nice features they are. But we're hoping that more people than just the organizer and the existing volunteers will access this site. We want to make it easy for visitors to find an event in their area, or one related to their favorite technology. If we stumbled upon a site like this, the first thing we'd do is search for *Groovy* or *Grails*. Let's add this type of search feature to TekDays.

We could create a search form with fields for all the searchable properties, and then we could use the Criteria Builder to dynamically build a query based on the user's input—but that would be kind of lame. What we'll do instead is provide a single search field on our home page, and we'll search for all possible matches to the value entered in that field. To do this, we'll take advantage of one of the most powerful plugins in the Grails ecosystem; the Searchable plugin[2] takes the indexing and search capabilities of Compass and Lucene and makes them easy to use. It makes them so easy, in fact, that we call it "Grails-easy."

Before we dig into this feature, let's talk about Grails' plugins. At last check, there are more than 900 plugins in the main repository. You can see what plugins are available by running grails list-plugins. The documentation for most

---

2. Developed by Maurice Nicholson; see http://grails.org/plugin/searchable.

Figure 44—TekDays home page with volunteer events

of them is at the main plugin portal: http://grails.org/plugins/. To install a plugin, we simply declare it as a dependency in BuildConfig.groovy. (We can get the dependency that we need to declare from the plugin's page in the plugin portal; the dependency for the Searchable plugin, for example, is listed at http://grails.org/plugin/searchable.)

Plugins seamlessly add features to a Grails application. They can add new domain classes, controllers, tag libraries, services, and more. Often, plugins wrap an existing Java library or framework, like the Twitter4J plugin,[3] which wraps the Twitter4J library.[4]

It's important to note that any library or framework that is provided by a plugin could be included directly in your application without the plugin. You could include the .jar files and write your code directly against the APIs. The point of plugins and the philosophy that most plugin authors have embraced is that these external libraries should be as easy to work with as Grails itself; plugin authors tend to follow the principle of preferring convention to config-uration but allowing configuration when it's desired.

The Searchable plugin allows us to perform full-text searches on all of the properties of our domain classes—even relationship properties. Let's take it for a spin. Open TekDays/grails-app/conf/BuildConfig.groovy and add the following highlighted line:

seek.1.2/TekDays/grails-app/conf/BuildConfig.groovy
```
plugins {
    // plugins for the build system only
    build ":tomcat:7.0.42"

    // plugins for the compile step
    compile ":scaffolding:2.0.1"
    compile ':cache:1.1.1'
    compile ":webxml:1.4.1"
    compile ":searchable:0.6.6"

    // plugins needed at runtime but not for compilation
    runtime ":hibernate:3.6.10.2" // or ":hibernate4:4.1.11.2"
    runtime ":database-migration:1.3.5"
    runtime ":jquery:1.10.2"
    runtime ":resources:1.2.1"

    // Uncomment these (or add new ones) to enable additional resources capabilities
    //runtime ":zipped-resources:1.0.1"
    //runtime ":cached-resources:1.1"
    //runtime ":yui-minify-resources:0.1.5"
}
```

Now we will start modifying our code to enable search. Let's start with Tek-Days/grails-app/domain/com/tekdays/TekEvent.groovy. Open it, and add the highlighted code:

---

3.   http://grails.org/plugin/twitter4j
4.   http://twitter4j.org/en/index.html

seek.1.2/TekDays/grails-app/domain/com/tekdays/TekEvent.groovy
```groovy
package com.tekdays

class TekEvent {
    String city
    String name
    TekUser organizer
    String venue
    Date startDate
    Date endDate
    String description
    String toString(){
      "$name, $city"
    }
    static searchable = true
    static hasMany = [volunteers : TekUser,
                      respondents : String,
                      sponsorships : Sponsorship,
                      tasks : Task,
                      messages : TekMessage]

    static constraints = {
        name()
        city()
        description maxSize: 5000
        organizer()
        venue()
        startDate()
        endDate()
        volunteers nullable: true
        sponsorships nullable: true
    }
}
```

"What?!" you say—"Only one line?!" That was our initial reaction, too. But it's true. That single line of code, static searchable = true, enables full-text search of all the simple properties of the TekEvent. Let's put this newfound power to use by adding a search action to our TekEventController. Open TekDays/grails-app/controllers/com/tekdays/TekEventController.groovy, and add the following action:

seek.1.2/TekDays/grails-app/controllers/com/tekdays/TekEventController.groovy
```groovy
def search = {
    if(params.query){
        def events = TekEvent.search(params.query).results
        [events : events]
    }
}
```

In this action, we start off with an if block to protect against a blank search. Then we have two lines: the first calls the search() method that the Searchable plugin has added to the TekEvent class, passing in the search query (which will come from a form we will be creating shortly). The search() method returns a SearchResult instance, which contains a results property that is a List. The next line just returns that list in a Map. This action will, by convention, attempt to render a view in a file called search.gsp, so let's give it one to render.

Joe asks:
What If We Want to Search Associated Objects?

At times, you may need to search for objects based on the properties of related objects. The Searchable plugin makes this easy also. Let's say, for example, that you want to be able to search for TekEvent instances based on the properties of their organizer or volunteers. These are both of type TekUser, so add this line to the TekUser class:

```
static searchable = true
```

Now go to the TekEvent class, and change that searchable declaration to look like this:

```
static searchable = {
        organizer component: true
        volunteers component: true
}
```

All you did was turn TekUser into a *searchable* class. Then you used the Searchable plugin's mapping DSL to tell it that the organizer and volunteers properties are *searchable components*. Notice that you don't have searchable = true anywhere in the TekEvent class; assigning a mapping closure to the searchable property automatically sets it to true.

There's a great deal more that can be done with the Searchable plugin—much more than we can cover here. Fortunately, you can find extensive documentation at http://grails.org/plugin/searchable.

Create an empty file called TekDays/grails-app/views/tekEvent/search.gsp, and add the following code:

seek.1.2/TekDays/grails-app/views/tekEvent/search.gsp
```html
<html>
  <head>
    <meta http-equiv="Content-Type" content="text/html; charset=UTF-8"/>
    <meta name="layout" content="main" />
    <title>Tek Event Search Results</title>
  </head>
  <body>
    <div class="nav" role="navigation">
      <ul>
        <li><a class="home" href="${createLink(uri: '/')}">Home</a></li>
      </ul>
    </div>
    <div id="list-tekEvent" class="content scaffold-list" role="main">
```

```
      <h1>Search Results</h1>
      <br />
      <ol class="property-list tekEvent">
        <g:if test="${events}">
          <g:each in="${events}" var="event">
            <li>
              <g:link action="show" id="${event.id}">${event}</g:link>
            </li>
          </g:each>
        </g:if>
        <g:else>
          <h3>No Matching Results Found</h3>
        </g:else>
      </ol>
    </div>
  </body>
</html>
```

The first part of this view is pretty much a copy of any of the other views we've created so far. After the "Search Results" heading, we create an ordered list. Next, we check to see whether we have any events. If we do, we use a <g:each> tag to iterate over the events and create a hyperlink list item for each one. If we don't have any events, we render an appropriate message.

At this point, we could actually run this code and begin searching, but we could do so only from the browser address bar with something like this: *http://localhost:8080/TekDays/tekEvent/search?query=perl*. That's rather stone-age.

Instead, let's add a proper search field to our home page. Open TekDays/grails-app/views/index.gsp, and add the highlighted code right after the "Welcome" paragraph.

seek.1.2/TekDays/grails-app/views/index.gsp

```
    <h3>Welcome to TekDays.com</h3>
    <p>TekDays.com is a site dedicated to assisting individuals and
      communities to organize technology conferences.  To bring great
      minds with common interests and passions together for the good
      of greater geekdom!</p>
  </div>
➤ <div id="homeSearch">
➤   <g:form controller="tekEvent" action="search">
➤     <label>Search:</label>
➤     <input id="query" type="text" name="query" />
➤     <input type=submit value="Go" />
➤   </g:form>
➤ </div>
```

We are using a <g:form> that will post to the search action of the tekEvent con-troller, and we have a single input element called query that will contain the search value. Finally, we have a submit element to fire it off. We're almost done.

If we were to run this now, it would work, but we would be prompted to log in when we tried to perform a search. We want everyone to be able to find events on our site, so we'll have to fix this.

The security check is happening in our security filter, so we will modify it to allow the search action. Open TekDays/grails-app/conf/SecurityFilters.groovy, and add "search" to the allowedActions list, as shown in the following code.

```
seek.1.2/TekDays/grails-app/conf/SecurityFilters.groovy
class SecurityFilters {
    def filters = {
        doLogin(controller:'*', action:'*'){
            before = {
                if (!controllerName)
                    return true
➤               def allowedActions = ['show', 'index', 'login',
➤                                     'validate', 'search']
                if (!session.user && !allowedActions.contains(actionName)){
                    redirect(controller:'tekUser', action:'login',
                            params:['cName': controllerName,
                                    'aName':actionName])
                    return false
                }
            }
        }
    }
}
```

Great! Now when we load our home page, it looks like what we see in Figure 45, *TekDays home page with search,* on page 160. Go ahead and try it. You can find events based on location, venue, name, and description. Our customer can find all the Groovy, Grails, and Griffon-related conferences that his heart desires. We're sure he'll be happy.

Summary

In this iteration, we added some useful features for event organizers, volun-teers, and users at large. Along the way, we learned about the Criteria Builder for involved queries and about the Searchable plugin for full-text search. We also got some more practice using those awesome Grails custom tags. The application is starting to look good and perform all kinds of handy functions.

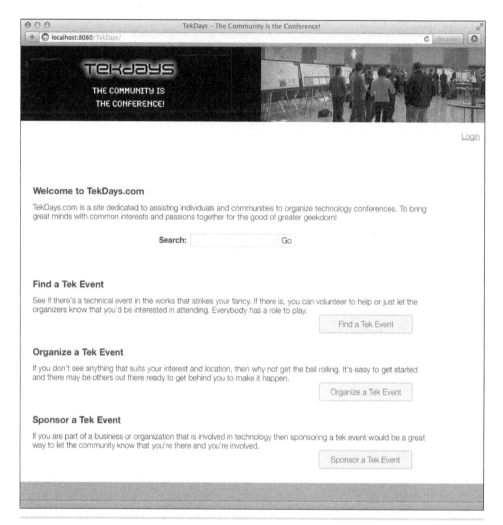

Figure 45—TekDays home page with search

Our customer is anxious to put it to use and is already preparing some ideas for version 1.1.

In the next chapter, we'll add volunteer registration and do some general refactoring based on feedback from our customer. We'll try more plugins and test some cool tricks with Grails URL mapping.

CHAPTER 11

Icing on the Cake

We are almost at the end of our project, and it is looking good. The customer is happy with our work, but he had a couple new feature requests. It happens. No worries, though. Because of the increased productivity of Grails and your own killer coding skills, we are ahead of schedule, so we should be able to fit these features in. Besides, that will give us the opportunity to try some more Grails plugins.

Let's take a look at what remains from our original feature list, and then we'll see whether we can fit in the extra goodies the customer asked for. We have only one item left from the first list:

- Allow access to event home page with simple URL

That shouldn't take too long. We should be able to get that done and also these new features:

- Make it easier for a user to volunteer for an event
- Provide a way for organizers to post news about event

Those sound like good ideas. With most other frameworks, this would be too much to take on in the time we have left, but with Grails, we can *code boldly*.

The jQuery UI Plugin

The first item on the new list is really just an improvement on one of the original features. We did provide a way for people to volunteer to help on events, but it's not very user friendly. So, we'll tackle this one right away. We'll add a button to the TekEvent show view that will allow logged-in users to volunteer to help on this event. When they click it, we'll show them a nice confirmation dialog box, and if they confirm, we'll add them to the volunteers collection for that event.

We'll start with the button. At first, that would seem as simple as adding a <button> tag somewhere on our page. But there is some logic involved. We don't want to show the button if the user is not logged in. Then if they are logged in, we don't want to show the button if they are already volunteering for this event. (Hopefully you can see where we're heading with this.) We could do this with a couple of <g:if> tags, but our guilty consciences might drive us to depression. So instead, we will put this logic into a custom tag.

Open TekDays/grails-app/taglib/com/tekdays/TekDaysTagLib.groovy, and add the following tag closure:

```
icing.2/TekDays/grails-app/taglib/com/tekdays/TekDaysTagLib.groovy
def volunteerButton = {attrs ->
    if (request.getSession(false) && session.user){
        def user = session.user.merge()
        def event = TekEvent.get(attrs.eventId)
        if (event && !event.volunteers.contains(user)){
            out << "<span id='volunteerSpan' class='menuButton'>"
            out << "<button id='volunteerButton' type='button'>"
            out << "Volunteer For This Event"
            out << "</button>"
            out << "</span>"
        }
    }
}
```

If a user is logged in, there will be a TekUser in the session called user, so that's our first test. If we have a logged-in user, we'll call the merge() method on it. (We need to do this because objects stored in the session become detached from the Hibernate session.) Then we use the eventId attribute to get the TekEvent instance. Once the user has been merged, we can pass it to the contains() method of the event.volunteers to see whether this user is already a volunteer. If they are not, we'll go ahead and write out the button. We start with a <span> with a class of menuButton and id of volunteerSpan. Note this id; it will become important shortly.

Next we write out the <button> with its id and type, followed by the text of the button. We finish by closing up all our tags.

Now we'll drop this tag in the navigation bar on the TekEvent show view, in TekDays/grails-app/views/tekEvent/show.gsp.

```
icing.2/TekDays/grails-app/views/tekEvent/show.gsp
<div class="nav" role="navigation">
  <ul>
    <li><a class="home" href="${createLink(uri: '/')}">
      <g:message code="default.home.label"/></a></li>
```

```
    <li><g:link class="list" action="index"><g:message
      code="default.list.label" args="[entityName]" /></g:link></li>
    <li><g:link class="create" action="create"><g:message
      code="default.new.label" args="[entityName]" /></g:link></li>
    <li><g:link class="list" controller="dashboard" action="dashboard"
      id="${tekEventInstance.id}"> Event Dashboard</g:link></li>
    <li><g:volunteerButton eventId="${tekEventInstance.id}" /></li>
  </ul>
</div>
```

When a logged-in user views an event that they are not currently volunteering for, the menu bar will look like the following figure.

Figure 46—TekEvent show view menu with volunteer button

That looks good, but it doesn't do anything yet. Let's fix that next. What we want is a confirmation dialog box, followed by a call to an action that will add this user to the volunteers collection of this TekEvent. Since we don't want a boring JavaScript dialog box, we'll use the jQuery UI plugin to get a much more attractive one.

The jQuery UI plugin[1] includes jQuery UI[2] resources (CSS and JavaScript) in our GSP pages, making it simpler to work with the library in a Grails application. Some of the components included in jQuery UI are Autocomplete, Tabs, Progressbar, and the one we're going to use, Dialog. To install the plugin, add the following dependency to the list of compile step plugins in TekDays/grails-app/conf/BuildConfig.groovy:

```
compile ":jquery-ui:1.8.24"
```

1. http://grails.org/plugin/jquery-ui
2. You can find very detailed documentation on jQuery UI at http://jqueryui.com/.

We are now ready to add the dialog box component to our TekEvent show view. Back in TekDays/grails-app/views/tekEvent/show.gsp, go ahead and add the highlighted lines to the <head> section:

icing.2/TekDays/grails-app/views/tekEvent/show.gsp

```
<head>
  <meta name="layout" content="main">
  <g:set var="entityName" value="${message(code: 'tekEvent.label',
    default: 'TekEvent')}" />
➤  <g:javascript library="jquery" />
➤  <r:require module="jquery-ui" />
  <title><g:message code="default.show.label"
    args="[entityName]" /></title>
</head>
```

Just as we saw in *Ajax in Grails*, on page 112, the <g:javascript> tag here is declaring the JavaScript library that we're using. (The jQuery UI plugin depends on the jQuery plugin,[3] which is included in our app automatically by Grails.) The <r:require> tag is being used to tell Grails' Resources framework that we are using the jquery-ui module provided by the jQuery UI plugin.

Next, we need to add the code for the jQuery UI dialog component. Add the following code right before the closing </body> tag:

icing.2/TekDays/grails-app/views/tekEvent/show.gsp

```
<script type="text/javascript">
    $(document).ready(function() {
        $('#volunteerDialog').hide();
        $( "#volunteerButton" ).click(function() {
            $("#volunteerDialog").dialog({
                resizable: false,
                height:180,
                width: 420,
                modal: false,
                buttons: {
                    "Submit": function() {
                        $.ajax({
                            type: "post",
                            dataType: "html",
                            url: "${g.createLink(action:'volunteer')}",
                            async: false,
                            data: $("#volunteerForm").serialize(),
                            success: function (response, status, xml) {
                                $("#volunteerSpan").html(response);
                            }
                        });
```

---

3. http://grails.org/plugin/jquery

```
                $(this).dialog("close");
            },
            Cancel: function() {
                $(this).dialog( "close" );
            }
        }
    });
});
});
</script>
<div id="volunteerDialog" title="Volunteer for ${tekEventInstance.name}">
  <g:form name="volunteerForm" action="volunteer">
    <g:hiddenField name="id" value="${tekEventInstance.id}" />
    <p>Welcome to the team! Your help will make a huge difference.</p>
  </g:form>
</div>
```

Note how easy Grails makes it for us to add JavaScript to a GSP. Our new JavaScript code here is using jQuery UI to show and hide a simple volunteerDialog <div>, which contains a <g:form> with a hidden input for the id of our event. The form's action attribute is set to volunteer, which is the name of the TekEventController action that we will use to add the logged-in user to this event's volunteers.

OK. Our dialog box is all set up. We could even run this now and it would show up, but we would just get a nasty error in the console if we tried to submit. Let's create the volunteer action in TekDays/grails-app/controllers/com/tekdays/TekEventController.groovy, like so:

`icing.2/TekDays/grails-app/controllers/com/tekdays/TekEventController.groovy`
```
def volunteer = {
    def event = TekEvent.get(params.id)
    event.addToVolunteers(session.user)
    event.save()
    render "Thank you for Volunteering"
}
```

The volunteer action is the heart of this feature, even though it's only a few lines of code. First we use the id that was passed in the hidden input field to get the TekEvent instance. Then we add the logged-in user (session.user) to the volunteers collection. Next, we save the event, and finally, we render a text message that will replace the button in the volunteerSpan. This action is a great example of how the productivity of Grails doesn't come in scaffolding or code generation; it comes in the way you are able to accomplish so much with so little code. Scaffolding helps out as you start a new application, but this ability to enhance and expand your application quickly is where the real productivity gains come in.

Let's see our new feature in action. Log someone in to the application, and navigate to an event that they haven't volunteered for. Click the button, and you should see something like the following figure. It's so easy that no one has an excuse for not volunteering.

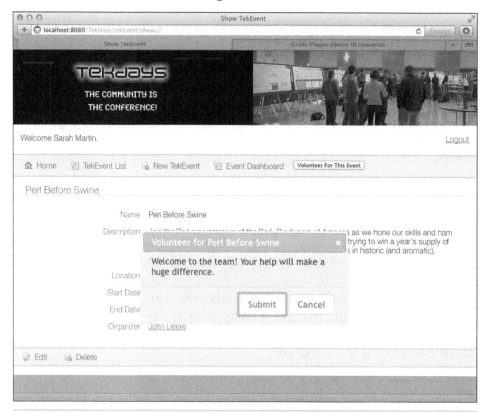

Figure 47—The volunteer dialog box

The Twitter4J Plugin

It seems that everyone is on Twitter[4] these days—even if they can't tell you why. We'll take advantage of this fact to help our hardworking event organizers get the word out about their events. If an event's organizer creates a Twitter account for their event, we will provide a form on the dashboard that will enable them to post updates to their event's Twitter timeline. To do this, we'll use the Twitter4J plugin mentioned earlier.

---

4. http://twitter.com

The Twitter4J plugin gives us easy access to the Twitter4J library.[5] In Tek-Days/grails-app/conf/BuildConfig.groovy, add the following dependency:

```
compile ":twitter4j:0.3.2"
```

This plugin provides a service class (Twitter4jService) that gives us access to the Twitter4J API,[6] which has a host of methods that interact with Twitter. We'll be using only a couple of these methods; you can read about the rest of them in the API documentation at http://twitter4j.org/javadoc/index.html.

Before we get started with the plugin, we need to set up our app as a Twitter client. To do this, go to https://dev.twitter.com/apps/new and sign in with a Twitter account. Fill out the required fields and click the "Create your Twitter application" button. On the page for our new Twitter application, look for the "Consumer key" and "Consumer secret". We will use these to give our app access to the Twitter API.

Run the TekDays application and navigate to http://localhost:8080/TekDays/twitter4j. Enter the two values that we obtained from our Twitter application page. The plugin will give you instructions on how to finish setting it up. (It even includes a view from which we can send a test tweet, so we can make sure we've configured everything correctly.)

Now we'll put the Twitter4jService to use. We'll add a new action to the Dashboard-Controller, because we're going to expose this feature in the organizer's dashboard. Open TekDays/grails-app/controllers/com/tekdays/DashboardController.groovy, and add the following code:

icing.2/TekDays/grails-app/controllers/com/tekdays/DashboardController.groovy
```
package com.tekdays

class DashboardController {

    def twitter4jService
    //Existing dashboard code snipped

    def tweet = {
        def event = TekEvent.get(params.id)
        if (event){
            twitter4jService.updateStatus(params.status)
        }
        redirect(action:dashboard, id:event.id)
    }
}
```

---

5. http://twitter4j.org/en/index.html
6. http://twitter4j.org/javadoc/

Note that we are defining a property called twitter4jService at the top of the class. When we declare that property using the convention of changing the first character of the class name to lowercase, Grails will inject a Twitter4jService instance into our controller at runtime. Next we add our tweet action, which starts out by getting the current TekEvent instance. If we have a valid instance, we call updateStatus(), which takes a latestStatus to post, on the Twitter4jService. That's all there is to it! Most of the other available methods are just as simple, and perhaps for version 1.1 we can add more Twitter integration since it's so easy to do. But for now, this gives us just what we need. Finally, we redirect to the dashboard so they can do it all over again.

Now we'll add a new section to the dashboard to call this action. Open Tek-Days/grails-app/views/dashboard/dashboard.gsp, and add the highlighted code:

```
icing.2/TekDays/grails-app/views/dashboard/dashboard.gsp
      <div id="sponsors" style='margin:10px 10px 10px 10px'>
        <g:render template="sponsors" model="${[sponsorships:sponsorships]}" />
      </div>
➤     <div id="twitter" style='margin:10px 10px 10px 10px'>
➤       <g:render template="twitter" model="${[event:event]}" />
➤     </div>
    </body>
</html>
```

We're going to put the specifics of our Twitter feature in a template, which we'll render in the dashboard view. Create a blank file called TekDays/grails-app/views/dashboard/_twitter.gsp, and add the following code:

```
icing.2/TekDays/grails-app/views/dashboard/_twitter.gsp
<h3>Post Event Updates to Twitter</h3>
<g:form name="twitterForm" action="tweet" id="${event.id}">
  (No more than 140 characters)<br/>
  <textarea name="status" rows="3" columns="50" style="width:100%;
    height:60"></textarea>
  <br/>
  <input type="submit" value="Post to Twitter" />
</g:form>
```

Our Twitter template uses <g:form> to create a form that will post to the tweet action and pass the event.id. We have only one input in our form: a <textarea> called status. This will contain the status message to post to Twitter. We finish the form with a standard submit button. Now we're ready to tweet!

In the following figure, we can see the bottom half of the dashboard view, which includes our new Twitter section. To test this, you can enter your own Twitter credentials and post a message starting with "@daveklein" or "@fifth-position". We'll let you know if it worked.

Forum Messages

Author	Subject	Content
John Doe	Can anyone recommend a good screen printer?	I need to get a quote on ...
Sarah Martin	I think I can get James Gosling to do a keynote	I know a guy who knows a ...
John Doe	Welcome to the Gateway Code Camp Forum	Welcome to the Gateway Co ...

View threaded messages for this event.

Sponsors

Name	Web Site	Contribution
Object Computing Incorporated	http://ociweb.com	Venue
Contegix	http://www.contegix.com	Other

Post Event Updates to Twitter

(No more than 140 characters)

Post to Twitter

Figure 48—Section of dashboard view with Twitter form

User-Friendly URLs

We now need to provide a way to access our event page using a simple URL. The way it stands now, once the application is deployed, the URL to a specific event's page looks something like this:

http://TekDays.com/tekEvent/show/5024753

(OK, the id might not be quite that large at first, but we're thinking positive here.) Our customer would like us to get to something more like http://Tek-Days.com/events/MyTekEvent. This will make it easier for the event organizers and volunteers to plaster links all over the Internet for their event.

As we have come to expect, Grails provides a simple way to do this. Every Grails application has a UrlMappings class, which uses a DSL[7] to build URL mappings. The conventional Grails mappings are in there by default, and we can add as many different mappings as needed. Let's take a look at the default

---

7. Domain-specific language.

mappings to get an idea of how this works. Open TekDays/grails-app/conf/UrlMappings.groovy:

```groovy
class UrlMappings {

    static mappings = {
        "/$controller/$action?/$id?(.${format})?"{
            constraints {
                // apply constraints here
            }
        }

        "/"(view:"/index")
        "500"(view:'/error')
    }
}
```

The static mappings block is the heart of the UrlMappings class. Inside this block we see the mappings for the conventional Grails behavior. The first value found after the root (/) will be assigned to the controller variable. The next value will be assigned to the action, and the one after that will be assigned to the id. (In the case of using file extensions for content negotiation, a file extension—which would then be the last value—would be assigned to the format variable.) The first variable, controller, is required; the rest have a ? on the end, which marks them as optional. What this means is that any URL with one, two, three, or four values after the root (including a file extension) will match this mapping and be applied accordingly. If we were to create a FooController, /foo would be mapped to the FooController's default action, /foo/bar would be mapped to the bar action of FooController, and /foo/bar/baz would be mapped to the bar action of FooController with an id parameter of baz. You get the picture.

Inside the mapping block there is an empty constraints block, where we can put constraints on the different variables, much as we did earlier on domain class properties. After this, we have the two other default mappings. The root mapping, when nothing but the application root is in the URL, maps directly to the index view. Mapping directly to a view makes sense for pages that don't need any data; for example, you might use this for an About page. Last of all, we have the 500 error mapping.

Let's add another mapping that will match the URLs that we want to support. The code should look something like this:

icing.2/TekDays/grails-app/conf/UrlMappings.groovy
```groovy
"/events/$nickname"{
    controller = "tekEvent"
    action = "show"
}
```

The default Grails mapping uses all variables. Our mapping is using a static value (events) and a variable ($nickname). Since our mapping does not include variables for controller and action, we need to set those inside the mapping block. This mapping will match any URL that starts with the word events and has one more value, which will be assigned to the variable $nickname. The matched URL will be directed to the show action of TekEventController with a nickname parameter. So, now we need our controller to make use of the nickname.

We're going to modify the show action to use a nickname parameter to show a TekEvent instance. Before we do that, though, we need to add a nickname to TekEvent. In TekDays/grails-app/domain/com/tekdays/TekEvent.groovy, add the two high-lighted lines below:

icing.2/TekDays/grails-app/domain/com/tekdays/TekEvent.groovy

```groovy
package com.tekdays
class TekEvent {
    String city
    String name
    TekUser organizer
    String venue
    Date startDate
    Date endDate
    String description
    String nickname
    String toString(){
      "$name, $city"
    }

    static searchable = true
    static hasMany = [volunteers : TekUser,
                      respondents : String,
                      sponsorships : Sponsorship,
                      tasks : Task,
                      messages : TekMessage]
    static constraints = {
        name()
        city()
        description maxSize: 5000
        organizer()
        venue()
        startDate()
        endDate()
        volunteers nullable: true
        sponsorships nullable: true
        tasks nullable: true
        messages nullable: true
        nickname nullable: true
    }
}
```

Now that we have that property, let's get to work. Open TekDays/grails-app/con-trollers/com/tekdays/TekEventController.groovy, and modify the show action like this:

```
icing.2/TekDays/grails-app/controllers/com/tekdays/TekEventController.groovy
def show(Long id) {
    def tekEventInstance
    if(params.nickname){
        tekEventInstance = TekEvent.findByNickname(params.nickname)
    }
    else {
        tekEventInstance = TekEvent.get(id)
    }
    if (!tekEventInstance) {
        if(params.nickname){
            flash.message = "TekEvent not found with nickname ${params.nickname}"
        }
        else {
            flash.message = "TekEvent not found with id $id"
        }
        redirect(action: "list")
        return
    }
    [tekEventInstance: tekEventInstance]
}
```

This action's job is to pass a TekEvent instance to the show view. Here, we're beginning the action by declaring the tekEventInstance, and we're giving the action two different ways to retrieve it: by its id or by its nickname. To do this, we separate the variable *declaration* from the *assignment*. We use an if to decide whether to retrieve the instance by nickname or by id. If there's a nickname value in the params, we use the dynamic finder findByNickname(). Then, to make our error messages clearer in case we don't find an instance, we use another if block to determine the appropriate error message to display.

We added the nickname of "GatewayCode" to one of our test events, so now we can navigate to http://localhost:8080/TekDays/events/GatewayCode to view the home page of the event.

Summary

We did it! We completed the original feature list for TekDays and even added a couple of bonus features with the time we saved by using Grails. We also saw firsthand how powerful and easy to use Grails plugins are. (Be sure to browse the Grails plugin portal at http://grails.org/plugins/ to see what others are available.)

All that's left to do now is to deploy the application to our server. Before you start thinking "Ant and Ivy and Maven, oh my!" remember that this is *Grails* we're talking about. Well, you'll see. Turn the page.

CHAPTER 12

Deployment and Beyond

We are nearing the end of our project and our time together. We've accomplished quite a bit, and our customer is happy with the results. He's also very impressed with how quickly we got it done. He's just about ready for us to hand the application over to him, but he wants us to try deploying it first—sort of as a sanity check.

When we created the TekDays application, Grails automatically installed the Grails plugin[1] for Tomcat,[2] which is what we've been running the app in up until now. There are also Grails plugins for other servers; for example, there is a plugin for Jetty, which is an HTTP server and Java servlet container. Some people do use Jetty for production deployment, but usually production will use something (such as Tomcat) that's a little more heavy-duty, or a full-blown JEE[3] server, such as WebLogic, JBoss, or, if they can't find a way out of it, WebSphere.

Grails applications will run well on any of these. For our purposes (and for most Grails applications), Tomcat is a good fit. We'll be sticking with it for our deployment here, but in place of it you can use any other standards-compliant Java servlet container you like.

Using a JNDI Data Source

Before packaging our application for deployment, we need to change our data source. Open TekDays/grails-app/conf/DataSource.groovy.

When we last worked on this file, it looked something like this:

---

1. http://grails.org/plugin/tomcat
2. http://tomcat.apache.org/
3. Java Enterprise Edition

> **Joe asks:**
> ## JEE Server, Java Servlet Container: What's the Difference?
>
> *JEE server* and *Java servlet container* are often used almost as interchangeable terms. They aren't the same thing, but they are related. A *JEE server* is an application server that implements the JEE specification. This specification includes things like EJB, JMS, JPA, JTA, JSP, Servlets, JSF, and more. (Don't worry if you don't recognize all of these.)
>
> A *Java servlet container* usually supports a subset of those JEE components, such as JSP, Servlets, and JSF—basically the web-related JEE components. Some servlet containers are gradually taking on more components, so these lines are beginning to blur.
>
> A simple way to look at it is that a servlet container is a lightweight JEE server.

```
dataSource {
    pooled = true
    driverClassName = "com.mysql.jdbc.Driver"
    username = "dave"
    password = "1234"
}
hibernate {
    cache.use_second_level_cache = true
    cache.use_query_cache = false
    cache.region.factory_class =
      'net.sf.ehcache.hibernate.EhCacheRegionFactory' // Hibernate 3
//    cache.region.factory_class =
//      'org.hibernate.cache.ehcache.EhCacheRegionFactory' // Hibernate 4
}

// environment specific settings
environments {
    development {
        dataSource {
            dbCreate = "update" // one of 'create', 'create-drop',
                                // 'update', 'validate', ''
            url = "jdbc:mysql://localhost:3306/tekdays"
        }
    }
    test {
        dataSource {
            dbCreate = "update"
            url = "jdbc:h2:mem:testDb;MVCC=TRUE;LOCK_TIMEOUT=10000"
        }
    }
```

```
    production {
        dataSource {
            dbCreate = "update"
            url = "jdbc:h2:prodDb;MVCC=TRUE;LOCK_TIMEOUT=10000"
            properties {
                maxActive = -1
                minEvictableIdleTimeMillis=1800000
                timeBetweenEvictionRunsMillis=1800000
                numTestsPerEvictionRun=3
                testOnBorrow=true
                testWhileIdle=true
                testOnReturn=false
                validationQuery="SELECT 1"
                jdbcInterceptors="ConnectionState"
            }
        }
    }
}
```

Our focus now is on the production block toward the end of the file. It currently points to an in-memory H2 database. It may seem obvious, but there *have* been incidents where applications went into production this way. It's not a good thing. So, we're going to make sure we get this changed.

Now, we could change the production dataSource to point to a MySQL instance, as we did for the development dataSource, but in most organizations it's considered bad form to include database credentials in an application configuration file. All JEE servers and virtually all Java servlet containers support the Java Naming and Directory Interface (JNDI).[4] And at the risk of once again sounding like a broken record: Grails makes it incredibly easy to use a JNDI data source.

Our customer studied up on the subject at http://tomcat.apache.org/tomcat-7.0-doc/jndi-datasource-examples-howto.html and has configured a JNDI data source in his Tomcat server named TekDaysDS. To direct our application to use that data source, we'll change the production block of DataSource.groovy like this:

deploy.2/TekDays/grails-app/conf/DataSource.groovy
```
production {
    dataSource {
        jndiName = "java:comp/env/jdbc/TekDaysDS"
    }
}
```

That's all there is to it. The exact layout of the JNDI string may vary with different servers, so if you're working with something other than Tomcat, refer

---

4.   http://docs.oracle.com/javase/7/docs/technotes/guides/jndi/index.html

to your server's documentation for more details. The production database URL and credentials will now be read from the server. The default values will still be used for the development and test environments.

Creating and Deploying a WAR

The standard way to deploy a Java-based web application is as a web application resource (WAR) file. There are many tools available to help package a web application into a WAR, from IDEs such as Eclipse and NetBeans to build tools such as Ant and Maven. With Grails, however, those things are rarely needed. A simple Grails script will do it for us.

```
$ grails war
```

That single script will compile our source code, pull in our dependencies, and bundle it all into a standard JEE WAR file. For our project, the default name for this file is TekDays-0.1.war. Deploying this to Tomcat is as simple as copying the file to Tomcat's webapps directory and restarting.

Our app deploys successfully on Tomcat. We're good to go...for now. No software application is ever really done; TekDays may be ready to start using, but it can always be improved.

Next Steps

We're sure that as we've worked on this project, you've thought of features that would be nice to have in TekDays, or perhaps different ways to implement features. Go for it! With the rapid feedback and flexible, dynamic nature of Grails, it's easy to explore and experiment.

You could look through the list of Grails plugins at http://grails.org/plugins/ and see which ones might be useful—and perhaps add a regional event calendar, or use the Grails mail plugin[5] to add email services to the application. Or you may have noticed that we don't yet have any facility for speakers or sessions. (Our customer was mostly interested in organizing open spaces conferences.)

But before you get too carried away with changes to this production system, there are a couple of things to consider: version control and database migration.

As stated earlier, Grails makes experimentation fun and easy, but you don't want to experiment with production code. You also don't want to start making duplicate project directories all over the place. So first of all, move the project into a version control system such as SVN or Git (the Grails source code itself

---

5.   http://grails.org/plugin/mail

is in Git). You can find information about using these systems with Grails at http://www.grails.org/Checking+Projects+into+SVN.

A database migration tool can help prevent database nightmares as you begin making changes to the database to implement new features. The Grails Database Migration plugin integrates the Liquibase[6] framework with Grails, helping you avoid those nightmares and rest easy as you migrate your database from version to version.

Feel free to take our application in different directions or to just borrow ideas from it and start something new. If you do something cool with it, let us know, and we'll feature it at http://gquick.blogspot.com.

Parting Thoughts

Now, feeling a bit like Mr. Rogers at the end of the show, it's time for us to take off our customer hat, our project manager hat, and our development team member hat and to put on our author hats. The goal of this book was to give you, the reader, a hands-on tutorial of web development with Grails: to demonstrate enough features and provide enough practice to get you past the newbie stage and on your way to mastery. It's our hope that you've learned enough to be productive with Grails. Even more, we hope that you caught a vision of the power, productivity, and pleasure of Grails.

Because this was a quick-start guide and not an in-depth reference, there are areas that we only touched on and where more information would be helpful. To that end, we've included an appendix that lists books, articles, websites, and blogs that will help you dig deeper. In the appendix, we'll also introduce you to the GR8 community.[7] The community is truly one of the biggest strengths of these technologies.

Finally, we hope you learned as much and had as much fun working through this book as we had writing it.

---

6. http://www.liquibase.org
7. GR8 refers to Groovy, Grails, Griffon (a Groovy desktop application framework inspired by Grails), and other Groovy-based tools and frameworks.

Additional CSS Rules

Here are some style rules that we have added to TekDays/web-app/css/main.css. Please copy these to your project to make it easier to follow along with the project in the book.

```css
/*Dashboard*/
.dashItem {
    margin: 10px;
}
#eventBlurb {
    width: 100%;
    height: 60px;
}
#dashHeader {
    text-align: center;
}


/*Index*/
#homeSearch {
    margin-left: 30%;
    margin-top: 25px;
    width: 40%;
}
#homeSearch label {
    font-weight: bold;
}
#welcome {
    margin-left: 25px;
    width: 85%;
}

.homeCell {
    margin-left: 25px;
    margin-top: 65px;
    width: 85%;
}
```

```css
.homeCell .buttons {
    width: 180px;
    text-align: center;
    float: right;
    margin-right: 30px;
    margin-bottom: 30px;
}

h3, li {
    margin-bottom: 15px;
}

/*Message Create*/
.messageField {
    width:550px
}

/*Ajaxlist*/
#messageList {
    margin: 20px 30px;
    overflow:auto
}

#messageList p {
    margin: 10px 0;
}

#show-message {
    margin: 20px 30px;
}

#detailHeading {
    margin-left: 30px;
    margin-bottom: 15px;
}

/*Volunteer Dialog*/
#volunteerDialog .ui-widget-header {
    color: #ABBF78;
    background-image: none;
    color: #000;
}
```

Resources

Now that you're up and running with Grails, you'll want to learn more, and you will undoubtedly have questions. What follows is a Grails resource guide, and then some. Since Grails is part of the greater GR8 community (pun entirely intended), this guide will point you to resources beyond Grails alone. These are the resources that we've used and/or that are made available by people who we know and respect; we trust that you'll find them useful as well.

Online Resources

The Internet has more than you'll ever need to know about most things, Groovy and Grails included. The following is a (very abbreviated) list of general websites and mailing lists that are worth checking out.

Grails: A Quick-Start Guide Blog . . . . http://gquick.blogspot.com
Additional tips, tricks and tutorials that build on the example from the book.

Official Grails website . . . . http://grails.org

Official Groovy website . . . . http://groovy.codehaus.org

Official Griffon website . . . . http://griffon.codehaus.org
Griffon is an MVC framework for rich desktop development with Groovy.

The Grails plugin portal . . . . http://grails.org/plugins/
A gold mine of plugin information. Besides a complete list of the plugins, there's documentation, tutorials, screencasts, and more. Tags and a rating system help you determine whether a plugin is right for you and help you choose between competing plugins.

Grails mailing lists . . . . http://grails.org/Mailing+lists
The Grails user and dev lists are quite active and loaded with helpful people. Don't be afraid to ask for help, and as you get more comfortable with the framework, don't be afraid to offer help. It's a great feeling when you go from just asking questions to answering them too.

Groovy mailing lists . . . . http://groovy.codehaus.org/Mailing+Lists
Sometimes your question will be more Groovy language-specific. When this happens, the folks on this list are quick to help. Also, if you are new to Groovy, taking some time to read through the threads on this list is a great way to learn more about the language.

GroovyBlogs . . . . http://groovyblogs.org
This is an excellent blog aggregator currently covering more than 350 blogs related to Groovy technologies.

Meet the GR8 Community

We've heard many people say this, and we wholeheartedly agree: one of the best things about Groovy, Grails, Griffon, and other Groovy tools is the community. The developers involved in these technologies are some of the smartest, most enthusiastic, and most helpful people we've worked with. We've had the pleasure of meeting many of them in person at various conferences; others we know only through the ether. But we consider it an honor to work with and be associated with them. Here's an introduction to some of your new colleagues.

The Grails Dev Team

Graeme Rocher . . . . http://grails.io
Graeme is the Grails project lead and a coauthor of *The Definitive Guide to Grails [Roc06]* and *The Definitive Guide to Grails 2*.

Marc Palmer . . . . http://grailsrocks.com
Marc is a Grails committer and has written many popular Grails plugins.

Dierk König http://www.manning.com/koenig2/
Dierk is a Grails committer and the lead author of *Groovy in Action [Koe13]*.

Jason Rudolph . . . . http://jasonrudolph.com
Jason is a Grails committer and a coauthor of *Getting Started with Grails* [Rud07].

Jeff Brown . . . . http://javajeff.blogspot.com
Jeff is a Grails committer and coauthor of *The Definitive Guide to Grails* and *The Definitive Guide to Grails 2*.

Marcel Overdijk . . . . http://marceloverdijk.blogspot.com
Marcel is a Grails committer and author of several Grails plugins.

Sergey Nebolsin . . . . http://snebolsin.blogspot.com
Sergey is a Grails committer and is the author of the Quartz plugin, among others.

Lee Butts . . . . http://www.leebutts.com
Lee is a Grails committer, plugin contributor, and car buff.

Burt Beckwith: An Army of Solipsists . . . . http://burtbeckwith.com/blog/
Burt is a Grails committer, a prolific plugin author, and a regular on the Grails mailing lists. Burt also served as the technical editor for the book *Grails in Action* and is the author of *Programming Grails*.

The Grails Podcast Team

Sven and Glen are the hosts of the Grails Podcast. For details, see *Other Media*, on page 187.

Sven Haiges . . . . http://hansamann.wordpress.com
Sven is the founder of the Grails Podcast.

Glen Smith . . . . http://blogs.bytecode.com.au/glen/
Glen is the creator of GroovyBlogs.org and coauthor of *Grails in Action [SL09]*.

Other GR8 Bloggers

There are currently over 350 blogs aggregated on GroovyBlogs.org. We're not going to list them all here, but these are some members of the community who have made (and are making) significant contributions. Their blogs are a rich source of information and experience, as well as a way to get to know them. When you come across them later on the mailing list or bump into them at a conference, it'll be like seeing an old friend.

Andres Almiray . . . . http://www.jroller.com/aalmiray/
Andres is a Groovy committer, a member of the core Griffon development team, a Grails plugin developer, and coauthor of *Griffon in Action [AFS2]*.

Hamlet D'Arcy: Behind the Times . . . . http://hamletdarcy.blogspot.com
Hamlet is a Groovy committer and AST wizard.

Peter Delahunty: Delahuntyware . . . . http://blog.peterdelahunty.com
Peter has written several Grails plugins and blogs frequently about his experiences, among other things.

Michael Easter: Code To Joy . . . . http://codetojoy.blogspot.com
Michael is a longtime Groovyist and software composer, well-known in the GR8 community for his Groovy (and related) insights shared at *Code To Joy*.

James Ervin: Iacobus . . . . http://iacobus.blogspot.com
James is the Groovy Eclipse plugin project lead and the creator of the Groovy Monkey Eclipse plugin.

Shawn Hartsock: Thoughts and Ideas . . . . http://hartsock.blogspot.com
Shawn is an enterprise Groovy and Grails expert, Grails plugin author, and contributor to *GroovyMag*.

Mike Hugo . . . . http://piraguaconsulting.blogspot.com
Mike is a Grails plugin author and contributor to *GroovyMag*. He has a lot of helpful information on his blog.

Hubert Klein Ikkink: Messages from mrhaki . . . . . http://mrhaki.blogspot.com
Mr. Haki, as he is known to GR8 developers everywhere, is another frequent blogger on Groovy and related topics. He is the author of the popular "Goodness" blog series, including "Groovy Goodness," "Grails Goodness," "Griffon Goodness," and "Gradle Goodness."

Chris Judd: Judd Solutions . . . . http://juddsolutions.blogspot.com
Chris is an author, speaker, trainer, and all-around Groovy guy. He is a coauthor of *Beginning Groovy and Grails: From Novice to Professional [SNJ08]*.

Ken Kousen: Stuff I've Learned Recently... . . . . . http://kousenit.wordpress.com
Ken is a Java and Groovy trainer and conference speaker. He is the author of *Making Java Groovy [Kou13]*.

Guillaume Laforge . . . . http://glaforge.appspot.com
Guillaume is the Groovy project manager, a coauthor of *Groovy in Action*, and a frequent conference speaker.

Tomás Lin: Programming Brain Dump . . . . http://fbflex.wordpress.com
Tomás is a Grails/Flex expert and author of the online book *Flex on Grails*.

Ted Naleid . . . . http://naleid.com/blog
Ted is a Grails plugin author and *GroovyMag* contributor.

**Josh Reed: Josh (formerly) in
Antartica** . . . . http://josh-in-antarctica.blogspot.com
Josh is a desktop Groovy pro and an up-and-coming Griffon power user.

Jim Shingler: Shingler's Thoughts . . . . http://jshingler.blogspot.com
Jim is a coauthor of *Beginning Groovy and Grails: From Novice to Professional* and a Griffon plugin author.

Matt Stine . . . . http://www.mattstine.com
Matt is a Grails plugin contributor, a Java user group leader, frequent conference speaker, and Groovy/Grails blogger.

Venkat Subramaniam . . . . http://blog.agiledeveloper.com
Venkat is an internationally recognized speaker and trainer and the author of *Programming Groovy 2: Dynamic Productivity for the Java Developer*.

James Williams . . . . http://jameswilliams.be
James is a Grails committer and member of the core Griffon development team.

**Dave Klein: Kickin' Down the
Cobblestones** . . . . http://dave-klein.blogspot.com
You can also reach me at daveklein@usa.net or on Twitter at http://twitter.com/daveklein.

Ben Klein . . . . http://benkle.in
Also find me at ben@silver-chalice.com, or, on Twitter, at http://twitter.com/fifthposition.

Other Resources

Besides blogs, websites, and mailing lists, there are many other resources available to new Grails developers. There are books, magazines, podcasts, screencasts, and training organizations.

Books

The shelves are filling up with Groovy and Grails books these days (well, at least ours are). Here are some of the more recent titles.

Grails in Action [SL09], **by Glen Smith and Peter Ledbrook** . .
. . . . http://manning.com/gsmith
A second edition (http://manning.com/gsmith2/) is expected to be in print in December 2013.

The Definitive Guide to Grails 2 [Roc12], **by Graeme Rocher and Jeff Brown** http://www.apress.com/9781430243779

Programming Groovy 2 [Sub13], **by Venkat Subramaniam** . .
. . . . http://pragprog.com/book/vslg2/programming-groovy-2

Making Java Groovy [Kou13], **by Ken Kousen** . .
. . . . http://www.manning.com/kousen/

Groovy Recipes [Dav08], **by Scott Davis** . .
. . . . http://www.pragprog.com/book/sdgrvr

Beginning Groovy and Grails [SNJ08], **by Judd, Shingler, and Nusairat** http://www.apress.com/book/view/9781430210450

Grails Persistence [Fis09], **by Robert Fischer** http://www.apress.com/book/view/1430219262

Groovy and Grails Recipes [Jaw08], **by Bashar Abdul Jawad** . .
. . . . http://www.apress.com/book/view/143021600x

Groovy in Action [Koe13], **Second Edition, by Köenig *et al.*** . .
. . . . http://www.manning.com/koenig2

Griffon in Action [AFS2], by Almiray, Ferrin and Shingler . .
. . . . http://www.manning.com/almiray/

Other Media

GroovyMag . . . . http://groovymag.com
A monthly e-magazine devoted to Groovy, Grails, Griffon, and other GR8 technologies.

The Grails Podcast . . . . http://grailspodcast.com
Sven Haiges and Glen Smith host a biweekly (or as they say, fortnightly) podcast with news, interviews, and interesting discussions centered around the GR8 community and technology.

Grails Screencasts . . . . http://grails.org/screencasts
Grails.org hosts a growing collection of screencasts on topics ranging from Ajax to JMX to the Grails Mail plugin.

Training

Even with all of these resources at our disposal, there are times when having an experienced instructor there to help you dig in can make a big difference. Don't worry; you're covered there as well. Here are training opportunities offered by some of the brightest minds in the business.

SpringSource Training http://www.springsource.com/training/grv001

ThirstyHead . . . . http://thirstyhead.com/

GroovyMag Online Training . . . . http://www.groovymag.com/training

IDE Support

As mentioned in *Setting Up Our Workspace*, on page 16, many Grails developers find that they don't need an integrated development environment (IDE) as much as they did when working with Java or other "high-ceremony" languages. In fact, an IDE sometimes gets in the way. A good text editor, a good browser, and the command line are often all you need to be productive with Grails. Personally, I (Dave) use TextMate; Ben, along with my former co-worker Nate (who happens to be the best programmer in the world), uses Vim.

That's not to say that there isn't support in the major IDEs. It's just to let you know that you may not need it once you get going. The three major Java IDEs —Eclipse, NetBeans, and IntelliJ IDEA—all have varying degrees of support for Groovy and Grails. NetBeans and IDEA seem to leapfrog each other as the top GR8 IDE, but SpringSource is actively working on its SpringSource Tool Suite's support, so by the time you read this, they may have leapt to the front. Here are links to information on the support in each IDE.

Eclipse and SpringSource Tool Suite (STS)

Grails STS integration . . . . http://www.grails.org/STS+Integration

Groovy Eclipse plugin . . . . http://groovy.codehaus.org/Eclipse+Plugin

NetBeans

Grails NetBeans integration . . . . http://www.grails.org/NetBeans+Integration

Groovy NetBeans integration . . . . . http://groovy.codehaus.org/NetBeans+Plugin

An introduction to working with Grails in Netbeans . .
. . . . https://netbeans.org/kb/docs/web/grails-quickstart.html

IntelliJ IDEA

Grails IDEA integration . . . . http://grails.org/IDEA+Integration

JetBrains Official Groovy
page . . . . http://www.jetbrains.com/idea/features/groovy.html

JetBrains Official Grails
page . . . . http://www.jetbrains.com/idea/features/grails.html

Bibliography

[AFS2]   Andres Almiray, Danno Ferrin, and James Shingler. *Griffon in Action*. Manning Publications Co., Greenwich, CT, 2012 .

[Dav08]   Scott Davis. *Groovy Recipes: Greasing the Wheels of Java*. The Pragmatic Bookshelf, Raleigh, NC and Dallas, TX, 2008.

[Fis09]   Robert Fischer. *Grails Persistence with GORM and GSQL*. Apress, New York City, NY, 2009.

[HT00]   Andrew Hunt and David Thomas. *The Pragmatic Programmer: From Journeyman to Master*. Addison-Wesley, Reading, MA, 2000.

[Jaw08]   Bashar Jawad. *Groovy and Grails Recipes*. Apress, New York City, NY, 2008.

[Koe13]   Dierk Koenig. *Groovy In Action*. Manning Publications Co., Greenwich, CT, Second, 2013.

[Kou13]   Ken Kousen. *Making Java Groovy*. Manning Publications Co., Greenwich, CT, 2013.

[Roc06]   Graeme Rocher. *The Definitive Guide to Grails*. Apress, New York City, NY, 2006.

[Roc12]   Graeme Rocher. *The Definitive Guide to Grails 2*. Apress, New York City, NY, 2012.

[Rud07]   Jason Rudolph. *Getting Started with Grails*. InfoQueue, http://www.infoq. com, 2007.

[SL09]   Glen Smith and Peter Ledbrook. *Grails in Action*. Manning Publications Co., Greenwich, CT, 2009.

[SNJ08]   Jim Shingler, Joseph Faisal Nusairat, and Christopher M. Judd. *Beginning Groovy and Grails: From Novice to Professional.* Apress, New York City, NY, 2008.

[Sub13]   Venkat Subramaniam. *Programming Groovy 2: Dynamic Productivity for the Java Developer.* The Pragmatic Bookshelf, Raleigh, NC and Dallas, TX, 2013.

Index

SYMBOLS

$ character
  calling toString(), 129, 149
  Groovy expressions, 3
''' characters, declaring multi-line String, 33
* character
  filter wildcard, 125
  generate-all script, 59
-> character, closure parameters, 4
/ character, redirecting with, 128
; character, optional, 1
<< shortcut, 7–8
<=> shortcut, 7
== shortcut, 3
? character, safe navigation, 73
[] characters
  List, 6
  Set, 8
{} characters
  closures, 4
  Groovy expressions, 4

A

<a> tag, displaying events by organizer, 149
action attribute
  Ajax tags, 112
  links in show view, 73
  URL mapping, 170
  volunteer button, 165
actionName, 126
actions, see also index action; show action
  Ajax tags, 112

defined, 27, 61
filters, 125
overview, 60–66
add(), 7–8
addDefaultTasks(), 95–96, 100
addToTasks(), 96
addToVolunteers(), 45
after filter, 125
afterView filter, 125
Ajax, 108–115
allErrors, 54
allowedMethods property, 65
anchor tag
  creating links, 68, 129
  dashboard view, 139
And, joining properties in dynamic finders, 43
and block, search with Criteria Builder, 151
anonymous users
  logging in, 121
  registering, 46
Apache Commons project, 124
Apache Shiro, 121, 130
Apple icons, 67
application.properties file, 19
arguments, generate-all script, 59
aria-labelledby attribute, 72
as operator, 44
assert(), 8
assert statements, 3
asterisk
  filter wildcard, 125
  generate-all script, 59

attr parameter, custom tags, 116
authentication, see logging in/out
Authentication plugin, 121
author variable, message forum, 107, 110, 113, 119
autoboxed objects, 6
Autocomplete, 163
automated unit tests, 25
autoreloading, 16
autowiring, 96

B

<backward> tag, 117
bar camps, 12
before filter, 125
belongsTo property, 46, 50, 56
Between, joining properties in dynamic finders, 43
bidirectional one-to-many relationships, 46, 56
binding, 106
blank constraint, 54
blob, 49
blogs, Grails and Groovy, 101, 182–185
body parameter, custom tags, 116, 119
Boolean tag, 101
BootStrap.groovy
  many-to-many relationships, 52
  one-to-many relationships, 44
  one-to-one relationships, 40

respondent addresses, 47
test data, 32–35, 38, 82
bootstrapping test data, 32–35, 38, 82
brackets
    closures, 4
    List, 6
    Set, 8
Broken Window theory, 17
BuildConfig.groovy
    database configuration, 82
    installing plugins, 153
<button> tag, 162–166
buttons
    creating, 68
    login/out, 123
    message forum, 105, 109, 111, 114
    pagination, 71
    reply, 111, 114
    Twitter, 168
    volunteer, 161–166
byte[] variable, 49

C

C language, 1
Captchas, 121
CAS, 121
cascading deletes, 46, 56
checkbox, completion, 101
children variable, message forum, 119
city property, 23, 89, 137, 149
class="messageField", 107
classes
    declaration, 60
    named-args constructor, 3
closures
    custom tags, 117
    custom validation, 54
    defined, 4
    each(), 6–7
    sort(), 6
code
    create-app default, 18
    source, xii
codec classes, 19
collect(), 143
collections, see also respondents collection; volunteers collection
    about Groovy, 5–9

filtering with custom tags, 118
many-to-many relationships, 50–54
simple data types, 46
colors example, 7
columns
    edit and create views, 77
    list view, 29, 35, 40, 70
com.tekdays package, 22, 33
compareTo(), 7
comparison expression, 6
comparison operator, 7
Compass, 153
completed property, 100
concurrency, optimistic, 24
conf directory, 18
configuration
    convention over, x, 18–19, 79, 155
    create-app default, 18
    databases, 79–83
constraints
    about, 54
    custom, 54
    domain classes, 30
    inList, 52, 54
    list of built-in, 54
    logo property, 49
    <select> element, 52
    task list, 100
    URL mapping, 170
    validation, 30, 54
    website property, 49
constructor, named-args, 3
contains(), 143, 162
content, message forum, 110, 113, 140
content negotiation, 62
contributionType, 141
controller attribute
    Ajax tags, 112
    links in show view, 73
    URL mapping, 170
controllerName, filters, 126
controllers, see also dashboard action; index action; show action
    actions overview, 60–66
    Ajax tags, 112
    controllers directory, 18
    conventions, 135
    create action, 62
    creating, 27, 38, 49, 135

dashboard view, 135, 142–143
delete action, 65
edit action, 64
from generate-all script, 59–66
interceptors, 121, 125–129
link creation, 68, 73
list on home page, 17, 133
save action, 63, 96
service classes, 94
update action, 64
URL mapping, 170
controllers directory, 18
convention over configuration, x, 18–19, 79, 155
count(), 62
count variable, restricting messages to an event, 105
create (CSS class), 145
create action, 62
create view
    dates, 29, 90
    from dynamic scaffolding, 28
    form template, 77–79
    GSP code, 74
    message forum, 103–107, 114
    modifying, 90–93
    rendering with create action, 62
    restricting messages to an event, 106–107
    save action, 63
    sponsors, 49
create-app, 16–20
create-controller, 38, 135
create-domain-class, 21–23, 33, 37
create-integration-test, 98
create-service, 94
create-tag-lib, 116
createCriteria(), 151
createLink(), 68, 129, 145
<createLink> tag, 129, 145
creditCard constraint, 54
criteria blocks, nesting, 151
Criteria Builder, search with, 151–153
cross-site scripting attacks, 73

CSS
  dashboard menu, 145
  displaying text properties,
    72
  list view, 70
  login/out, 129
  main.gsp view, 67
  message forum, 107, 110
  modifying, 85
  show view, 72
  style rules, 85, 110, 179
  web-app directory, 19
curly braces, 4
custom constraints, 54
custom tags
  displaying events by orga-
    nizer, 148–150
  displaying events by vol-
    unteer, 152
  displaying message
    threads with, 116–120
  login/out, 128
  taglib directory, 19
  volunteer button, 162–
    166
custom validation, 54

D

dash-rocket, 4
dashboard action, 142–143
dashboard view, 131–146
  controllers, 135, 142–143
  designing, 135–141
  links, 138–139, 145
  menu, 143
  Twitter4J plugin, 166–
    168
DashboardController
  creating, 135
  dashboard action, 142–143
  linking to dashboard, 146
  Twitter4J plugin, 167
DashboardControllerSpec, creating,
  135
Database Migration plugin
  advantages, 177
  autoinstallation, 17
  migrations directory, 19
  resources, 82
databases
  changing for deployment,
    173–176
  configuring, 79–83
  migrations, 17, 19, 82,
    176
databases, in-memory
  advantages, 34

bootstrapping test data,
  32–35
development environment,
  16, 82
databases, persistent
  compared to in-memory
    databases, 34
  domain model and, 21
  production environment, 82
  test environment, 82, 99
DataSource.groovy
  changing for deployment,
    173–176
  configuring, 79–83
dates
  create view, 29, 90
  edit view, 90
  form template, 78
  list view, 71
  search, 151
  show view, 89
Davis, Scott, ix
DbdocController, 17
def index(), 27
def keyword, dynamic typing,
  3, 24
defaultEncodeAs, 117
delete action, 65
deletes, cascading, 46, 56
deployment, 173–176
description
  declaring multiline String,
    33
  form template, 77
  modifying in show view,
    89
  search, 151
details variable, message forum
  template, 110
development environment
  databases, 80, 82
  default, 16
Dialog, 163
dialog box, volunteer button,
  161–166
directories
  create-app, 16, 18
  dashboard, 135
  GSP, 19, 108
dollar sign
  calling toString(), 129, 149
  Groovy expressions, 3
doLogin filter, 126
domain classes
  adding properties, 23

adding tests, 24–27
constraints, 30
controllers and, 135
creating, 21–23, 33, 37–
  40
creating controller classes, 27
many-to-many relation-
  ships, 49–54
metaprogramming, 23
one-to-many relation-
  ships, 44–46
one-to-one relationships,
  40–44
domain directory, 18
domain model, 21
Don't Repeat Yourself principle, 94, 119
dot notation, Map, 8
DRY principle, 94, 119
dynamic finders
  limiting lists, 143
  missing methods, 41, 43
  search, 147–150
  URL mapping, 172
dynamic operators, 43
dynamic scaffolding
  advantages, 29
  constraints, 54
  controller creation, 27
  enabling, 38, 53
  generating code, 59
  GSP code, 66–79
  modifying views, 86–93
  one-to-many relation-
    ships, 44, 47
  views from, 28
dynamic typing, 3, 24–25

E

each()
  displaying events by orga-
    nizer, 149
  displaying message
    threads with custom
    tag, 118
  List, 6
  Map, 7
<each> tag
  dashboard view, 140–141
  form template, 79
  list view, 70
  message forum, 110,
    117, 140
  one-to-many relation-
    ships in show view, 73

search, 158
sponsors, 141
<eachError> tag, 74
echo, 15
Eclipse, 19, 176, 188
edit action, 64
edit view
   from dynamic scaffolding,
      28, 36
   form template, 77–79
   GSP code, 74
   modifying, 90–93
   task list checkbox, 101
   update action, 65
EJB, x
ellipsis, truncating with, 140
Ellison, Larry, 79
email addresses
   collecting, 46
   constraint, 54
   dashboard view, 139
   show view, 73
email constraint, 54
employee list example, 8
encodeAsForTags, 117
encodeAsHTML(), 71, 73, 90
endDate property, 89
Enterprise JavaBeans (EJB),
   x
environment variable, GRAILS
   _HOME, 14
equals(), with ==, 3
errors
   bootstrapping test data,
      33
   constraints, 54
   create view, 74
   form template, 77
   save action, 63
   update action, 65
   URL mapping, 170, 172
errors property
   bootstrapping test data,
      33
   constraints, 54
   create view, 74
event variable
   restricting messages to
      an event, 105
   URL mapping, 171
eventId attribute, 162
events, see also TekEvent
  class
   creating, 21–35

dashboard view, 137–
   141, 146
registering respondents,
   46
restricting messages to
   an event, 103–107
search with Criteria
   builder, 151–153
search with dynamic
   finders, 147–150
URL mapping, 171
exiting controller actions, 61
explicit declaration, 2
expressions
   designating, 3
   embedding, 138

F

Facebook Connect, 121
favicons, 67
feedback loop, 17
fieldValue(), 71
fieldcontain, 72
fields, accessing directly, 2
file input element, 49
filtering
   message forum, 103–
      107, 118
   security, 121, 125–129
findAll, 118
findAllByOrganizer(), 148
findAllByParent(), 119
findByFullName(), 41
findByName(), 45
findByNickname(), 172
findByUserName(), 124
flash
   login/out, 124
   message element, 69
   notFound() method, 66
   save action, 63
   update action, 65
flush:true, 63
<form> tag
   login/out, 127
   restricting messages to
      an event, 106
   search field, 159
   Twitter template, 168
   volunteer button, 165
form template
   modifying in create and
      edit view, 90
   rendering, 74

restricting messages to
   an event, 106
using, 77–79
form variable
   notFound() method, 66
   save action, 63
format attribute, 89
formats
   Boolean tag, 101
   content negotiation, 62
   dates, 71, 89
forms
   HTML, 74, 77–79
   login/out, 123, 127
   modifying in create and
      edit view, 90
   notFound() method, 66
   restricting messages to
      an event, 106
   save action, 63
   volunteer button, 165
forum, see message forum
frameworks
   plugins, 155
   support, x

G

<g:backward> tag, 117
<g:createLink> tag, 145
<g:datePicker> tag, 78, 90
<g:each> tag
   dashboard view, 140–141
   form template, 79
   list view, 70
   message forum, 110,
      117, 140
   one-to-many relation-
      ships in show view, 73
   search, 158
   sponsors, 141
<g:eachError> tag, 74
<g:form> tag
   errors, 74
   login/out, 123, 127
   search field, 159
   Twitter template, 168
   volunteer button, 165
<g:formatBoolean> tag, 101
<g:formatDate> tag, 71, 89
<g:hasErrors> tag, 74, 77
<g:hiddenField> tag, 76
<g:if> tag
   list view, 69

restricting messages to
an event, 107
show view, 72
<g:javascript> tag, 112, 164
<g:layoutBody> tag, 67
<g:layoutHead> tag, 67
<g:layoutTitle> tag, 67
<g:link> tag
about, 68
dashboard view, 139, 145
form template, 79
message forum reply
button, 111
restricting messages to
an event, 105
show view, 73
<g:message> tag
about, 70
link creation, 68
save action, 63
<g:organizerEvents> tag, 148
<g:paginate> tag, 71
<g:remoteLink> tag, 112, 117
<g:render> tag, 74, 108, 136
<g:select> tag, 77
<g:sortableColumn> tag, 70
<g:textArea> tag, 77, 107
<g:textField> tag, 107
<g:volunteerEvents> tag, 152
generate-all script, 59, 135
get()
dashboard action, 142
explicit declaration, 2
getters, 2
GORM
about, 41
restricting messages to
an event, 105
GR8 community, 177, 182–
185
Grails
advantages, ix–xi
installing, 14, 19
resources, 112, 153,
177, 181–188
Resources framework,
67, 164
tools, 19
versions, xii
grails command, scripts, 15
Grails Database Migration
plugin
advantages, 177
autoinstallation, 17

migrations directory, 19
resources, 82
Grails Object Relational Mapping, see GORM
grails-app directory, 18
GRAILS_HOME environment variable, 14
grailsw shell script, 19
grailsw.bat batch file, 19
Griffon, 181
Groovy
about, xii, 1
closures, 4
collections, 5–9
compared to Java, 1–3
expressions, 3, 138
GString, 3
installation, 1
List class, 5–7
Map class, 5, 7
metaprogramming fea-
tures, 9, 23, 43
resources, 1, 9, 101,
120, 181–188
Set class, 5, 8
tools, 19
tutorial, 1–10
Groovy In Action, 1
Groovy Server Pages, see GSP
GroovyMag, 120, 187
GSP
create view code, 74
custom tag, 116–120
directories, 19
edit view code, 74
from generate-all script, 59
home page makeover,
131–134
jQuery UI plugin, 163–
166
list view code, 68–71
logging in/out, 122
message forum, 108–120
methods from tags, 77,
119
show view code, 71–74
views code, 66–79
GString
about, 3
login/out, 129

H
Halloway, Stuart, 25
hasErrors(), 63, 65
<hasErrors> tag, 74, 77
hasMany property, 44, 46, 50

<head> tag, 67, 109
help
scripts, 15
testing installation, 14
Hibernate
configuration files, 18
familiarity with, xii
passing changes with
flush:true, 63
search with Criteria
Builder, 151–153
transactions, 95
<hiddenField> tag, 76
home (CSS class), 145
home page
changing logo, 85
default, 17
displaying events by organizer, 147–150
displaying events by vol-
unteer, 152
GSP code, 68–71
main.gsp view, 67
makeover, 131–134
search field, 153–159
simple URL, 161, 169–
172
Houston Tech Fest, 12
href attribute, 68
HTML
Ajax tags, 112
custom tags, 117
encodeAsHTML(), 71, 73, 90
forms, 74, 77–79
hidden field, 76
main.gsp view, 67
<select> element con-
straint, 52
HTTP
allowed methods, 65
redirect, 61, 124
status codes, 60, 63, 65
HttpStatus, 60
Hunt, Andy, 17

I
i18n, 19, 70
icons, main.gsp view, 67
id property
about, 24
Ajax tags, 112, 114
dashboard action, 142
restricting messages to
an event, 105
save action, 63

searching events by volunteer, 152
show action, 62
show view, 73
URL mapping, 170, 172
volunteer button, 162, 165
volunteers in dashboard view, 139
IDEs, 19, 176, 187
if, filters, 126
<if> tag
list view, 69
show view, 72
images, web-app directory, 19
import statement, including, 33
in-memory databases, *see* databases, in-memory
inList constraint, 52, 54
indent parameter, 119
index action
about, 27, 61
login/out, 124
message forum template, 114
notFound() method, 66
restricting messages to an event, 105
index.gsp, *see* home page
init(), bootstrapping test data, 32
install-templates script, 29
installation
Grails, 14, 19
Grails Database Migration plugin, 17
Groovy, 1
jQuery UI plugin, 163
plugins, 153
integration testing, *see* testing, integration
IntelliJ IDEA, 19, 188
interceptors, 121, 125–129
internationalization, 19, 70
Internet Explorer, 67
IsNotNull, 43
it parameter, 4, 6–7

J

jArrayList, 6
.jar files
lib directory, 19
plugins, 155

Java
advantages, ix
compared to Groovy, 1–3
Java servlet containers, 173–174
JNDI data source, 173–176
Java Database Connectivity, 42, 82
Java servlet containers, 173–174
java.util.ArrayList, 6
JAVA_HOME environment variable, 14
JavaScript
Ajax tags, 112
jQuery, 112, 161–166
web-app directory, 19
<javascript> tag, 164
JavaServer Faces (JSF), x
JBoss, 173
JDBC, 42, 82
JDK, JAVA_HOME environment variable, 14
JEE servers
compared to Java servlet containers, 174
deployment, 173–176
Jetty, 173
JNDI data source, deployment, 173–176
jQuery
library, 112
UI plugin, 161–166
JSF, x
JSON, 124
JUnit testing framework, 24, 98

K

key property, 7
key/value pairs
constraints, 30
hasMany property, 44
Map, 7
restricting messages to an event, 105

L

latestStatus, 168
layout
create view, 77
edit view, 77
main.gsp view, 67
left shift operator, add(), 7–8

left-margin, 119
LessThan, 43
<li> tag
displaying events by organizer, 149
show view, 72
task list, 97
lib directory, 19
libraries
Ajax tags, 112
lib directory, 19
list of supported, 112
plugins, 155
library attribute, Ajax tags, 112
Like, joining properties in dynamic finders, 43
links
creating, 68, 129
dashboard view, 138–140, 145
list view, 35, 68
login/out, 129
message forum, 105, 111, 117, 119
from search, 147–150
show view, 73
simple URL, 169–172
sponsors, 140
sponsorships, 79
task list, 138
volunteers, 139
Liquibase framework, 177
List
about, 5–7
filters, 126
order, 8
years attribute, 91
list(), parameters, 62
list (CSS class), 145
list variable, restricting messages to an event, 105
list view
with constraints, 30
default features, 35, 40
from dynamic scaffolding, 28
GSP code, 68–71
links, 35, 68
message forum, 105
modifying, 86
rendering with respond(), 62
with sample data, 34
TekUser, 39
list-plugins, 153

lists
    comma-separated, 73
    constraints, 52, 54
    CSS class, 145
    dashboard view, 137, 140
    email addresses, 73
    message forum, 103,
        110, 118
    multiselect, 78
    restricting messages to
        an event, 103
    scrolling, 110
    sponsors, 140
    sponsorships, 79
    task list, 94–101, 137,
        143, 145
literal declaration
    ArrayList default, 8
    List, 5
    Map, 7
locations, show view, 89
logging in/out
    dashboard view, 143
    displaying volunteers'
        events, 151–153
    setup, 121–129
    volunteer button, 161,
        165
loginToggle, 128
logo
    application in main.gsp
        view, 67
    changing, 29, 85
    sponsors, 49
Lucene, 153

M
main.gsp, 67
Making Java Groovy, 1
many-to-many relationships,
    creating, 49–54
Map
    about, 5, 7
    coercing, 43
    exiting controller actions,
        61
    named-args constructor,
        3
    params property, 61
    restricting messages to
        an event, 105
mapping, URLs, 169–172
matches constraint, 54
Math.min(), 61, 140
max(), 6
max constraint, 54, 61, 143

maxSize constraint, 30, 49, 54
menuButton, 162
merge(), 162
message bundles, 70
message element, flash, 69
message forum
    dashboard view, 139, 143
    displaying threads with
        custom tag, 116–120
    restricting messages to
        an event, 103–107
    setup, 54
    templates and Ajax calls,
        108–115
<message> tag
    about, 70
    link creation, 68
    save action, 63
messageList, 110
MessageThread tag, 117–120
<meta> tag, 67
metaClass, 9
metaprogramming
    about, 9
    domain classes, 23
    dynamic finders, 43
methodMissing(), 9
methods
    argument parameters, 62
    dynamic operators, 43
    filters, 125
    GSP tags, 77, 119
    metaprogramming basics,
        9
    missing, 9, 41, 43
    optional parentheses, 2
Microsoft Internet Explorer,
    67
migrations directory, 19
migrations, database, 17, 19,
    82, 176
min(), 6
min constraint, 54
minSize constraint, 54
mocking, 43
model
    index action, 62
    showDetail action, 113
Model View Controller frame-
    work, x
models, exiting controller ac-
    tions, 61
msg parameter, 118

multiline String, declaring with
    quotes, 33
multiple attribute, 78
multiselect listbox, 78
MVC4 framework, x
MySQL JDBC connector, 82

N
name property, displaying
    events by organizer, 149
named-args constructor, 3
names
    controllers, 135
    displaying events by orga-
        nizer, 149
    events in message forum,
        106
    events in show view, 88
    principle of least sur-
        prise, 21
    printing example, 6
    Set example, 8
    uppercase example, 3
nesting
    criteria blocks, 151
    message forum, 116–120
NetBeans, 19, 176, 188
Nicholson, Maurice, 153
nicknames, URL mapping,
    171
noSelection attribute, 78
notFound(), 63, 66
nullable constraint, 54
Nuxoll, Joe, 2

O
objects
    autoboxed, 6
    displaying related, 73
    searching, 157
offset element, 143
one-to-many relationships
    bidirectional, 46, 56
    creating, 44–46, 56
    domain classes, 44–46
    <g:select> tag, 78
    Set class default, 8
    show view, 73
    Strings, 44
one-to-one relationships, 40–
    44
Open Symphony, 66
OpenID, 121
optimistic concurrency, 24

Or, joining properties in dynamic finders, 43
or block, search with Criteria Builder, 151
order, *see also* sorting
  columns in list view, 35, 40, 70
  constraints, 30
  custom tags, 117
  List, 8
  list view, 29
  Set, 8
  task list, 143
order element, 143
organizer property
  changing, 40
  displaying related objects in show view, 73
  mocking with Map, 43
  modifying in show view, 89
  one-to-one relationships, 40–44
  removing from list view, 86
  search, 147–150
<organizerEvents> tag, 148
organizers
  dashboard view, 131–146
  removing from list view, 86
  search, 147–150
  setup, 40–44
  show view, 73, 89
  Twitter4J plugin, 166–168
ORM, 42
Overdijk, Marcel, 59
owning side, declaring, 50

P
packages, scripts, 22
pagination
  dashboard view, 143
  list view, 71
parameters
  closures, 4
  comparison expression, 6
  create action, 62
  custom tags, 116
  dashboard action, 142
  filters, 126
  index action, 61
  restricting messages to an event, 106

show action, 62
showDetail action, 113
params property
  create action, 62
  dashboard action, 142
  filters, 126
  index action, 61
  restricting messages to an event, 106
  show action, 62
  showDetail action, 113
parent property, message forum, 107, 114, 118
parentheses
  constraints, 30
  optional, 2, 96
passwords, 123–124, 177, *see also* security
persistent databases, *see* databases, persistent
Plain Old Groovy Object, 94
plugins
  about, 153
  Grails Database Migration plugin, 17, 19, 82, 177
  jQuery UI, 161–166
  listing, 17, 19, 153
  resources, 82, 153, 172, 176, 181
  search, 153–159
  security, 121, 130
  Twitter4J, 155, 166–168
POGO, 94
The Pragmatic Programmer, 17, 94
precision attribute, 78
principle of least surprise, 21
println(), 5
processMessages(), 118
production environment
  about, 16
  databases, 82
  deployment, 175
Programming Groovy 2, 1, 5, 10
Progressbar, 163
properties
  about, 2
  adding to TekEvent, 23
  application.properties file, 19
  constraints, 30
  displaying text, 72
  dynamic finders, 43
  filters, 126

form template, 77
list view, 35, 40
metaprogramming basics, 9
named-args constructor, 3
parentheses, 2
search, 153–159
property-label, 72
property-value, 72

Q
query element, 159
question mark, safe navigation with, 73
quotes
  declaring multiline String, 33
  GString, 3

R
<r:layoutResources> tag, 67
<r:require> tag, 67, 164
Range, years attribute, 91
ranges, truncating with, 140
readOnly element, omitting, 63
redirect()
  login/out, 124, 128
  save action, 63
redirecting
  controller actions, 61
  login/out, 124, 128
  save action, 63
  to home page, 149
regular expressions, constraint, 54
relationships
  many-to-many, 49–54
  one-to-many, 8, 44–46, 56, 73, 78
  one-to-one, 40–44
  search and, 151
reloading, auto-, 16
<remoteLink> tag, 112, 117, 119
render()
  exiting controller actions, 61
  login/out, 124
  message forum template, 113
<render> tag, 74, 108, 136
reply action, message forum, 111, 114
<require> tag, 67, 164

resources
  Grails, 112, 153, 177, 181–188
  Grails Database Migration plugin, 82
  Groovy, 1, 9, 101, 120, 181–188
  jQuery UI plugin, 163
  plugins, 82, 153, 172, 176, 181
  Searchable plugin, 157
  String class, 3
  Twitter4J plugin, 167
Resources framework, 67, 164
respond()
  create action, 62
  exiting controller actions, 61
  index action, 62
  save action, 63
  show action, 62
  update action, 65
respondents
  dashboard view, 137
  setup, 46
  show view, 73
respondents collection
  creating, 46
  dashboard view, 137
  show view, 73
results property, 156
return statements, optional, 1
reverse(), 116
role attribute, 67
root mapping, 170

S
safe navigation operator , 73
save()
  constraints, 54
  task list service class, 96
save action, 63, 96
scaffolding, *see* dynamic scaffolding
scope, flash, 63
screen readers
  aria-labelledby attribute, 72
  role, 67
scripting attacks, cross-site, 73
scripts
  about, 15
  create-controller, 38, 135

create-domain-class, 21–23, 33, 37
create-integration-test, 98
create-service, 94
create-tag-lib, 116
generate-all, 59, 135
grailsw shell, 19
install-templates, 29
packages, 22
scripts directory, 19
test-app, 26
war, 176
scripts directory, 19
scrolling, list, 110
search, 147–159
  Criteria Builder, 151–153
  dynamic finders, 147–150
  Searchable plugin, 153–159
search action, 156, 159
search() method, 156
search view, 156
Searchable plugin, 153–159
SearchResult, 156
security, 121–129
  cross-site scripting attacks, 73
  dashboard view, 143
  filters, 121, 125–129
  plugins, 121, 130
  search, 159
SecurityFilters, 125–129, 159
<select> element, 52, 77
semicolons, optional, 1
service classes
  authentication, 124
  services directory, 19
  task list, 94–100
serviceMethod(), 95
services directory, 19
session, 125
set, explicit declaration, 2
Set class, about, 5, 8
setters, 2
setup(), task list, 100
Shiro, 121, 130
show action
  about, 62
  dashboard view, 139
  URL mapping, 171
show view
  dashboard link, 145
  from dynamic scaffolding, 28, 36

GSP code, 71–74
links from search, 147–150
message forum, 103–106
modifying, 88–90, 103–106
one-to-many relationships, 45
one-to-one relationships, 42
rendering with show action, 62
respondents, 47
sponsorships, 53
task list, 97
URL mapping, 172
volunteer button, 161–166
showDetail action, 113
Silicon Valley Code Camp, 12
SiteMesh, 66
size(), 7
slash character, redirecting with, 128
sort(), List, 6
sort element, 143
SortedSet, 8
sorting, *see also* order
  columns, 35, 40, 70
  List, 6
  list view, 35, 40, 70
  task list, 143
<span> tag
  show view, 72
  volunteer button, 162
spinner image, 67
Spock
  integration tests, 98
  unit test class, 22
Sponsor class
  dashboard view, 140, 145
  diagram, 48
  many-to-many relationships, 49–54
  search, 152
  setup, 48–49
SponsorController, creating, 49
sponsors
  dashboard view, 140, 143, 145
  form template, 79
  modifying in show view, 90
  search, 152
  setup, 48–54

Sponsorship class
    dashboard view, 140, 143, 145
    diagram, 51
    form template, 79
    modifying in show view, 90
    search, 152
    setup, 51–54
SponsorshipController, creating, 79
Spring
    configuration files, 18
    familiarity with, xii
    Security, 121, 130
    transactions, 95
SpringSource, 188
square brackets, 6, 8
src directory, 19
startDate property, 71, 89, 151
static mappings, 170
status, Twitter plugin, 168
String
    collections and hasMany property, 46
    declaring multiline with quotes, 33
    domain classes as, 23
    quotes, 3
    resources, 3
    truncating with ranges, 140
strings
    blank constraint, 54
    collections and hasMany property, 46
    declaring multiline with quotes, 33
    GString, 3, 129
    quotes, 3
    truncating with ranges, 140
subject variable, message forum, 107, 110, 113, 119
submit button, 123
Subramaniam, Venkat, 5, 10
subscript operator, 6, 8
synthesizing behavior, 41, 43

T
tables, 137–140
Tabs, 163
TagLib class, 116–120, 148
taglib directory, 19

tags, *see also* custom tags
    library descriptors (TLDs), 117
    main.gsp view, 67
    taglib directory, 19
target directory, 19
Task
    dashboard view, 137, 143, 145
    default task list, 94–101
    diagram, 55
    modifying to show completion, 100
    setup, 54
    testing, 98–100
taskService property, 100
TaskService class, 95–97
TaskServiceSpec.groovy, testing, 99
<td> tag, 71
technical conferences, 12, 177, *see also* TekDays.com
tekdays database, creating, 82
TekDays.com
    about, 12
    creating, viewing, modifying events, 21–35
    customer, 12–14
    dashboard view, 131–146
    deployment, 173–176
    features list, 13
    home page makeover, 131–134
    login/out, 121–129
    message forum, 103–120
    modifying scaffolded views, 86–93
    relationships and domain classes, 37–57
    search, 147–159
    security, 121–129
    setup, 11–20
    simple URL, 169–172
    task list, 94–101
    Twitter4J plugin, 166–168
    views with GSP, 66–79
    volunteer button, 161–166
    workspace setup, 16–18
TekDaysDS, 175
TekEvent class
    adding tests, 24–27, 32–35
    bootstrapping test data, 32–35
    constraints, 30

    creating, 21–23, 62
    creating controller classes, 27
    dashboard action, 142–143
    dashboard view, 137–141, 146
    deployment, 173–176
    diagram, 22
    many-to-many relationships, 49–54
    modifying scaffolded views, 86–93
    one-to-many relationships, 44–46, 56
    one-to-one relationships, 40–44
    restricting messages to an event, 103–107
    save action, 63
    search, 147–159
    task list service class, 96
    views with GSP, 66–79
    volunteer button, 161–166
TekEvent.addToVolunteers(), 45
TekEvent.count(), 62
TekEvent.findByName(), 45
TekEvent.id, restricting messages to an event, 105
tekEvent.toString(), 26
TekEventController
    actions overview, 60–66
    creating, 27
    logging in/out, 124
    search action, 156
    task list service class, 96
    URL mapping, 171
TekEventInstance, save action, 63
tekEventInstanceCount, 62
tekEventInstanceList, 70
TekMessage
    diagram, 55
    displaying threads with custom tag, 116–120
    message forum template, 111
    restricting messages to an event, 103–107
    setup, 54
TekMessageController
    message forum template, 112
    restricting messages to an event, 105
tekMessageInstance, message forum template, 111

TekUser class
    controller, 38
    creating, 37–40
    dashboard view, 139
    diagram, 37
    logging in/out, 121–129
    one-to-many relation-
        ships, 44–46, 78
    one-to-one relationships,
        40–44
    search, 157
    test data, 38
    testing task list, 100
TekUserController
    creating, 38
    logging in/out, 122–129
    redirecting to home page,
        149
templates
    dashboard view, 136–141
    form, 74, 77–79, 106
    generate-all script, 59
    install-templates script, 29
    message forum, 108–115
    rendering GSP, 108
    Twitter, 168
ternary operator, 140
test addDefaultTasks(), 100
test directory, 19
test environment
    about, 16
    databases, 82, 99
test toString(), 26
test-app script, 26
TestFor annotation, 26
testing, see also testing, inte-
    gration; testing, unit
    databases, 82, 99
    domain classes, 24–27
    dynamic languages, 25
    installation, 14
    test directory, 19
    test-app script, 26
testing, integration
    task list service class, 98–
        100
    test directory, 19
    test-app script, 26
testing, unit
    creating unit test class,
        22
    domain classes, 25–27
    dynamic languages, 25
    one-to-one relationships,
        42

test directory, 19
test-app script, 26
text
    displaying CSS text prop-
        erties, 72
    form template, 77
    full-text search, 155–159
    message forum, 107
    render(), 124
    <textArea> tag, 77, 107
    Twitter, 168
<textArea> tag, 77, 107
<textarea> element, 77, 168
<th> tag, 70
Thomas, Dave, 17
times(), 5
<title> tag, 67
TLDs (tag library descriptors),
    117
toggle, login/out, 128
toList(), 8
Tomcat, deployment, 173–176
toString()
    adding to domain classes,
        23
    displaying events by orga-
        nizer, 149
    login/out, 129
    testing, 25
toUpperCase(), adding to domain
    classes, 3
<tr> tag, 70
@Transactional, 60, 63
transactions
    annotation, 60, 63
    service classes, 95
truncating messages, 140
tweet action, 168
Twitter4J plugin, 155, 161,
    166–168
types
    associating with hasMany
        property, 46
    optional, 3
    Set, 8
    specifying properties, 23

uber-generate-all, 59
unique constraint, 54
unit testing, see testing, unit
unit: flag, 26
update action, 64

update attribute, Ajax tags,
    112
updateStatus(), Twitter, 168
uppercase example, 3
uri, login/out, 128
url constraint
    defined, 54
    sponsors, 49
UrlMappings class, 169–172
URLs
    constraint, 49, 54
    controller actions, 61
    creating links, 68
    HTTP redirect, 61
    login/out, 128
    mapping, 169–172
    simple, 161, 169–172
    sponsors, 49
user, login/out, 124
userName, login/out, 143
username, login/out, 123, 128
utils directory, 19

V
validate(), constraints, 54
validate action
    login/out, 123, 127
    redirecting to home page,
        149
validation
    constraints, 30, 54
    login/out, 123, 127
    redirecting to home page,
        149
    save action, 63
validator constraint, 54
value property, each(), 7
version control, 176
version property, 24, 76
versions
    default for new applica-
        tions, 19
    Grails, xii
    JDK, 14
view parameter
    index action, 62
    message forum template,
        114
    save action, 63
views, see also create view;
    dashboard view; edit view;
    list view; show view
    controllers and, 135
    from dynamic scaffolding,
        28

exiting controller actions, 61
folder, 27
GSP code, 66–79
message forum, 103–115
modifying scaffolded, 86–93
render(), 124
search view, 156
using constraints to order display, 30
views directory, 19
views directory, 19
visitors, search, 153–159
volunteer action, 165
volunteer property, modifying in show view, 89
volunteerDialog, 165
<volunteerEvents> tag, 152

volunteerSpan, 162, 165
volunteers
dashboard view, 138, 143
log in/out, 143
modifying in show view, 89
search by event, 151–153
setup, 44–46
volunteer button, 161–166
volunteers collection
dashboard view, 138, 143
one-to-many relation-ships, 44–46
search by event, 151–153
volunteer button, 161–166
vsize constraint, 54

W
WAR files, creating and deploying, 176
web-app directory, 19
WebLogic, 173
website property, sponsors, 49
WebSphere, 173
wildcard, filters, 125
Windows, installation, 15
withFormat(), 63, 66
workspace setup for Tek-Days.com, 16–18
wrapper directory, 19

X
XML, 124

Y
years attribute, 91

Put the "Fun" in Functional

Elixir puts the "fun" back into functional programming, on top of the robust, battle-tested, industrial-strength environment of Erlang.

Programming Elixir

You want to explore functional programming, but are put off by the academic feel (tell me about monads just one more time). You know you need concurrent applications, but also know these are almost impossible to get right. Meet Elixir, a functional, concurrent language built on the rock-solid Erlang VM. Elixir's pragmatic syntax and built-in support for metaprogramming will make you productive and keep you interested for the long haul. This book is *the* introduction to Elixir for experienced programmers.

Dave Thomas
(240 pages) ISBN: 9781937785581. $36
http://pragprog.com/book/elixir

Programming Erlang (2nd edition)

A multi-user game, web site, cloud application, or networked database can have thousands of users all interacting at the same time. You need a powerful, industrial-strength tool to handle the really hard problems inherent in parallel, concurrent environments. You need Erlang. In this second edition of the best-selling *Programming Erlang*, you'll learn how to write parallel programs that scale effortlessly on multicore systems.

Joe Armstrong
(548 pages) ISBN: 9781937785536. $42
http://pragprog.com/book/jaerlang2

Seven Databases, Seven Languages

There's so much new to learn with the latest crop of NoSQL databases. And instead of learning a language a year, how about seven?

Seven Databases in Seven Weeks

Data is getting bigger and more complex by the day, and so are your choices in handling it. From traditional RDBMS to newer NoSQL approaches, *Seven Databases in Seven Weeks* takes you on a tour of some of the hottest open source databases today. In the tradition of Bruce A. Tate's *Seven Languages in Seven Weeks*, this book goes beyond your basic tutorial to explore the essential concepts at the core of each technology.

Eric Redmond and Jim R. Wilson
(354 pages) ISBN: 9781934356920. $35
http://pragprog.com/book/rwdata

Seven Languages in Seven Weeks

You should learn a programming language every year, as recommended by *The Pragmatic Programmer*. But if one per year is good, how about *Seven Languages in Seven Weeks*? In this book you'll get a hands-on tour of Clojure, Haskell, Io, Prolog, Scala, Erlang, and Ruby. Whether or not your favorite language is on that list, you'll broaden your perspective of programming by examining these languages side-by-side. You'll learn something new from each, and best of all, you'll learn how to learn a language quickly.

Bruce A. Tate
(330 pages) ISBN: 9781934356593. $34.95
http://pragprog.com/book/btlang

The Joy of Math and Healthy Programming

Rediscover the joy and fascinating weirdness of pure mathematics, and learn how to take a healthier approach to programming.

Good Math

Mathematics is beautiful—and it can be fun and exciting as well as practical. *Good Math* is your guide to some of the most intriguing topics from two thousand years of mathematics: from Egyptian fractions to Turing machines; from the real meaning of numbers to proof trees, group symmetry, and mechanical computation. If you've ever wondered what lay beyond the proofs you struggled to complete in high school geometry, or what limits the capabilities of the computer on your desk, this is the book for you.

Mark C. Chu-Carroll
(282 pages) ISBN: 9781937785338. $34
http://pragprog.com/book/mcmath

The Healthy Programmer

To keep doing what you love, you need to maintain your own systems, not just the ones you write code for. Regular exercise and proper nutrition help you learn, remember, concentrate, and be creative—skills critical to doing your job well. Learn how to change your work habits, master exercises that make working at a computer more comfortable, and develop a plan to keep fit, healthy, and sharp for years to come.

This book is intended only as an informative guide for those wishing to know more about health issues. In no way is this book intended to replace, countermand, or conflict with the advice given to you by your own healthcare provider including Physician, Nurse Practitioner, Physician Assistant, Registered Dietician, and other licensed professionals.

Joe Kutner
(254 pages) ISBN: 9781937785314. $36
http://pragprog.com/book/jkthp

Explore Cucumber and Automated Testing

Delve deep into Cucumber and beef up your automated testing with more Cucumber.

The Cucumber Book

Your customers want rock-solid, bug-free software that does exactly what they expect it to do. Yet they can't always articulate their ideas clearly enough for you to turn them into code. *The Cucumber Book* dives straight into the core of the problem: communication between people. Cucumber saves the day; it's a testing, communication, and requirements tool – all rolled into one.

Matt Wynne and Aslak Hellesøy
(336 pages) ISBN: 9781934356807. $30
http://pragprog.com/book/hwcuc

Cucumber Recipes

You can test just about anything with Cucumber. We certainly have, and in *Cucumber Recipes* we'll show you how to apply our hard-won field experience to your own projects. Once you've mastered the basics, this book will show you how to get the most out of Cucumber—from specific situations to advanced test-writing advice. With over forty practical recipes, you'll test desktop, web, mobile, and server applications across a variety of platforms. This book gives you tools that you can use today to automate any system that you encounter, and do it well.

Ian Dees, Matt Wynne, Aslak Hellesøy
(272 pages) ISBN: 9781937785017. $33
http://pragprog.com/book/dhwcr

Tinker, Tailor, Solder, and DIY!

Get into the DIY spirit with Raspberry Pi or Arduino. Who knows what you'll build next...

Raspberry Pi

The Raspberry Pi is a $35, full-blown micro computer that runs Linux. Use its video, audio, network, and digital I/O to create media centers, web servers, interfaces to external hardware—you name it. And this book gives you everything you need to get started.

Maik Schmidt
(149 pages) ISBN: 9781937785048. $17
http://pragprog.com/book/msraspi

Arduino

Arduino is an open-source platform that makes DIY electronics projects easier than ever. Even if you have no electronics experience, you'll be creating your first gadgets within a few minutes. Step-by-step instructions show you how to build a universal remote, a motion-sensing game controller, and many other fun, useful projects. This book has now been updated for Arduino 1.0, with revised code, examples, and screenshots throughout. We've changed all the book's examples and added new examples showing how to use the Arduino IDE's new features.

Maik Schmidt
(272 pages) ISBN: 9781934356661. $35
http://pragprog.com/book/msard

The Pragmatic Bookshelf

The Pragmatic Bookshelf features books written by developers for developers. The titles continue the well-known Pragmatic Programmer style and continue to garner awards and rave reviews. As development gets more and more difficult, the Pragmatic Programmers will be there with more titles and products to help you stay on top of your game.

Visit Us Online

This Book's Home Page
http://pragprog.com/book/dkgrails2
Source code from this book, errata, and other resources. Come give us feedback, too!

Register for Updates
http://pragprog.com/updates
Be notified when updates and new books become available.

Join the Community
http://pragprog.com/community
Read our weblogs, join our online discussions, participate in our mailing list, interact with our wiki, and benefit from the experience of other Pragmatic Programmers.

New and Noteworthy
http://pragprog.com/news
Check out the latest pragmatic developments, new titles and other offerings.

Save on the eBook

Save on the eBook versions of this title. Owning the paper version of this book entitles you to purchase the electronic versions at a terrific discount.

PDFs are great for carrying around on your laptop—they are hyperlinked, have color, and are fully searchable. Most titles are also available for the iPhone and iPod touch, Amazon Kindle, and other popular e-book readers.

Buy now at *http://pragprog.com/coupon*

Contact Us

Online Orders:	*http://pragprog.com/catalog*
Customer Service:	*support@pragprog.com*
International Rights:	*translations@pragprog.com*
Academic Use:	*academic@pragprog.com*
Write for Us:	*http://pragprog.com/write-for-us*
Or Call:	+1 800-699-7764

CPSIA information can be obtained at www.ICGtesting.com
Printed in the USA
LVOW02s2345140114

369398LV00020B/103/P

9 781937 785772